Instructor's Manual • Test Bank

for

COGNITIVE PSYCHOLOGY

Second Edition

Karl Haberlandt
Trinity College

Allyn and Bacon
Boston · London · Toronto · Sydney · Tokyo · Singapore

Copyright © 1997 by Allyn & Bacon
A Viacom Company
160 Gould Street
Needham Heights, Massachusetts 02194

Internet: www.abacon.com
America Online: keyword: College Online

All rights reserved. The contents, or parts thereof, may be reproduced for use with *Cognitive Psychology,* Second Edition, by Karl Haberlandt, provided such reproductions bear copyright notice, but may not be reproduced in any form for any other purpose without written permission from the copyright owner.

ISBN 0-205-26494-8

Printed in the United States of America

10 9 8 7 6 5 4 3 2 1   01 00 99 98 97 96

TABLE OF CONTENTS

Introduction

Course Information	1
Student Questions	6
Multiple-Choice Questions	23
Chapter 1. Introduction	23
Chapter 2. Cognitive Neuroscience	31
Chapter 3. Attention	40
Chapter 4. Recognition and Action	52
Chapter 5. Declarative and Procedural Knowledge	63
Chapter 6. Neural Networks	74
Chapter 7. Learning and Memory	86
Chapter 8. Working Memory	97
Chapter 9. Long-Term Memory	106
Chapter 10. Language: Structure and Meaning	115
Chapter 11. Language Comprehension	125
Chapter 12. Reading and Writing	137
Chapter 13. Problem Solving	147
Chapter 14. Reasoning and Choice	157
Chapter 15. Applications of Cognitive Psychology	167

INTRODUCTION

This manual includes information on a typical Cognitive Psychology course, a set of student questions, and a set of multiple choice questions for each chapter.

The Cognitive Psychology course assumes that students have completed a coursee in Introductory Psychology (Psychology 101). Two sample syllabi are included, one for courses based on the semester system and another for course using the quarter system. In each case, the 15 chapters of the text are mapped to fit within the weeks of the respective terms. The syllabi list the chapters in their order in the text; however, other sequences may be used as well. For example, an instructor may choose to treat the cognitive neuroscience chapter (Chapter 2) and neural network chapter (Chapter 6) toward the end of the term and use the following chapter sequence: 1, 3-5, 7-15, 2, and 6. Another option would be to discuss Chapter 7 with its historical perspective immediately after Chapter 1 for the following sequence: 1, 7, 2-6, 8-15.

The student questions provide a sense of student reactions to the material and alert the instructor to topics difficult for students, for example, the neural network approach in Chapter 6. I have taught from the text for three semesters and collected written student questions after completing each chapter, usually at the end of a class period. I would respond to the questions at the beginning of the next period, before launching into a new topic. This question and answer period yielded some dividends; it frequently developed into a lively debate about the current topic and about cognition in general.

In addition to conveying substantive content, one of the instructor's tasks is to evaluate student performance. I used several tools of assessing student performance, a term paper, multiple-choice tests, and class participation. The term paper is described in the syllabus. The multiple-choice tests include factual and conceptual questions. I tell students that for many questions, several alternatives seem correct and suggest that they choose the best fitting one. Occasionally this leads to debates with students, but that is how learning occurs (on both sides!). In my course, the typical testing period lasts 75 minutes and includes up to 60 questions. Most students finish well before time is up. Mean correct responses usually range between 40-45 correct answers. I return the tests to students as soon as practically feasible and provide class feedback on those questions where the largest number of errors occurred and on any other questions of interest.

I gratefully acknowledge the help of Elizabeth Adorno, Tyler Booth, Marsha Byrne, Lisa Galipo, Judy Kiely, Tracy Knight, Alex Mabilon, Jennifer Novak, Susan Roth, and Dawn Zorgdrager in preparing this manual. They assisted in composing multiple-choice questions, typing, and proofing the manuscript.

COURSE INFORMATION

Cognitive Psychology

Cognitive Psychology studies human information processing in its many manifestations: how people acquire, retrieve, and use information. Cognitive psychology is a broad field that includes several subdisciplines and is closely related to other disciplines as well. Cognitive psychologists pursue research on attention, perception, knowledge representation, learning, memory, language, and reasoning. Their research is increasingly dependent on advances in neuroscience, computer science, and linguistics. We shall discuss these related disciplines as well as some applications of cognitive principles throughout the semester.

The goals of the course are to
o familiarize you with the substantive content in the area of cognitive psychology
o expose you to some of the principal methods used in this field of study
o enable you to examine methodological and theoretical issues critically
o to enable and interest you to read the primary literature in cognitive psychology

1. Reading and class participation.
Assignments are indicated on the syllabus. Readings must be done prior to each lecture class. I expect that you will contribute to the class with interesting and pertinent questions. You will understand the materials best if you study the assigned readings a couple of times and summarize sections in writing. You will find it useful to edit your summaries after attending class.

2. Term paper
The paper is due during the final week of the term. See topics below.

3. Tests
There are three exams, including the final. The purpose of the exams is to review previous materials and to evaluate your performance. There will be a review session prior to each test.

4. Text.
Haberlandt, K. (1997) *Cognitive Psychology*. Boston: Allyn & Bacon.

Reading assignments are obligatory. Please note that readings and lectures are complementary. Not everything in the text can be covered in class, and some lecture topics are not treated in the text. Assigned readings should be done before each lecture class.

5. Grade.
Ninety per cent of your grade will be based on written work and ten per cent will be based on your contributions to the class discussions. Each test contributes 20% to your grade; the term paper accounts for 30%.

SYLLABUS (semester)

6. Reading Assignments (for weeks 1 - 13 enumerated on left)

Foundations of Cognitive Psychology

1	Philosophy, Linguistics, and Computer Science	Ch. 1
2	Neuroscience and Cognition	Ch. 2

Attention, Perception, and Action

2,3	Attention	Ch. 3
3	Recognition and Action	Ch. 4

Representation of Knowledge

4	Declarative and Procedural Knowledge	Ch. 5
4	Test 1 [Chapters 1 - 5]	
5	Parallel Architecture of Cognition	Ch. 6

Learning and Memory

6	History of Learning and Memory Research	Ch. 7
7	Working Memory	Ch. 8
8	Long-Term Memory	Ch. 9

Cognitive Skills

9	Language Structures and Language Processing	Ch. 10-11 (selections)
10	Test 2 [Chapters 6 - 10]	
10	Language Skills	Ch. 12
11	Problem Solving	Ch. 13
12	Problem Solving & Reasoning	Ch. 14
13	Applications of Cognitive Psychology	Ch. 15

Final exam period Test 3 [cumulative; emphasis on 11-15]

SYLLABUS (quarter system)

6. Reading Assignments (for weeks 1 - 10 enumerated on left)

Foundations of Cognitive Psychology

1	Philosophy, Linguistics, and Computer Science	Ch. 1
2	Neuroscience and Cognition	Ch. 2

Attention, Perception, and Action

3	Attention	Ch. 3
3	Recognition and Action	Ch. 4

Representation of Knowledge

4	Declarative and Procedural Knowledge	Ch. 5
4	Test 1 [Chapters 1 - 5]	
4,5	Parallel Architecture and Cognition	Ch. 6

Learning and Memory

5,6	History of Learning and Memory Research	Ch. 7
6	Working Memory	Ch. 8
7	Long-Term Memory	Ch. 9

Cognitive Skills

7,8	Language: Structures, Processing, and Skills	Ch. 10-12 (selections)
8	Test 2 [Chapters 6 - 10]	
9	Problem Solving & Reasoning	Ch. 13 - 14
10	Applications of Cognitive Psychology	Ch. 15

Final exam period Test 3 [cumulative; emphasis on 11-15]

Term Paper

Choose a topic for your term paper from the three topics listed below. Identify and read sources for each topic. Examine each topic carefully and make sure that you feel comfortable with it before committing yourself. The paper's suggested length is 12 typewritten pages written according to the format of the American Psychological Association (APA).

- <u>Cognition Applied.</u> Although Cognitive Psychology is a basic science that advances through laboratory research, the field has benefitted from insights gained through applications in the real world. Your paper should identify an application of cognitive principles, describe the application in detail, and report how the application has influenced theoretical and research developments in the field.
- <u>Affect and Memory.</u> Cognitive psychologists have focussed their attention on such rational functions as pattern recognition, learning, problem solving, and speech comprehension. The contribution of affect has largely been ignored. However, emotion and affect have played a role in the study of memory. Your paper is to review recent sources on the role of emotion in memory. You should seek to determine what scientists can learn about memory by studying the effects of affect on memory.
- <u>Motor Control.</u> Here is another important area that has been ignored for too long. Fortunately, there are many sources on motor control. The goal of your paper is to select an instance of motor control and examine its relation to cognition. Do they differ, and if so, how? Or are motor control and cognition similar, and if so, in what respects?

Use the first few weeks of the semester to collect sources, choose a topic, develop your ideas, and make an outline of your chosen topic and issues. The outline should enumerate the issues you plan to consider and include a list of the sources you are planning to use. Be sure to select issues for which sources are available at the College Library; experience has shown that the use of extramural resources leads to unnecessary delays. Your library research will yield many sources for each topic. You will need to be selective in several respects: choose specific problems within the general topic of your choice, discriminate between essential and tangential information, take a stand on issues, and select your arguments. These are choices every writer must face on his or her own. Once you have composed the outline reread each source until you feel comfortable with the points discussed by the author(s). Continue to refine the issues you wish to discuss. Then write several drafts before submitting the final version to me. I'll evaluate your paper on the basis of its creativity, organization, and style.

You can demonstrate your creativity in these ways: (1) Choose interesting and important issues for discussion. (2) Identify critical questions raised by the author(s). (3) Show your understanding and appreciation of those issues by stating them in your own words rather than by quoting the original (and don't plagiarize!) (4) Illuminate your topic by reference to related reading and class materials. You may criticize the author(s) if you think it is appropriate, but be sure to support your criticisms by evidence.

<u>Deadlines</u>
After Test 1 - Outline
Final Week - Paper due in class

Selected paper topics from other semesters
- <u>Control of cognition</u>

Comment: Cognitive psychology has made great advances in its understanding of the processes and structures of cognition. However, much less is known on whether there is an executive system that controls those processes and if so how the controlling system should be characterized. Recently, some proposals have surfaced. Search under such keywords as: control of action, attentional control, and executive control.

- <u>The role of consciousness in cognition</u>

Comment: William James considered consciousness as the subject matter of psychology. While behaviorist psychologists and even cognitive psychologists banished consciousness from consideration, it is currently making a comeback in the study of cognition. Your paper should address the role of conscious and of unconscious processes in cognition. Keywords: Implicit learning and memory, learning without awareness, perception without awareness.

- <u>Memory from a developmental perspective</u>

Comment: This topic calls for the examination of memory either for a specific age group or across groups, for example, infants, children, or the aged. Performance should be examined specifically as a function of age. While any memory paradigm is acceptable, whether it taps explicit or implicit memory, semantic or episodic memory, you should seek to find out what researchers can learn about memory by taking the developmental perspective.

STUDENT QUESTIONS

CHAPTER 1

1. Do cognitive psychologists believe that the mind works in the most efficient way possible when a person works on a particular task? Although the concept of mental efficiency is very important, cognitive psychologists typically do not treat it in their theories. Rather the implicit assumption is that people tend to do their best when working on a task. In the chapter on attention, however, we shall see that experimenters seek to influence a person's efficiency by using different payoff schemes for his or her performance. Efficiency comes also into play when we discuss expertise in certain skills, for example, in Chapter 5. Experts have extended practice in a particular domain and their performance is relative fast and free of errors.

2. Do the Gestalt principles also apply to language so that when a person utters an ungrammatical expression the listener is able to fill in what's missing? Certain Gestalt principles, for example, the principle of closure, apply to language. Studies of speech perception have shown that listeners fill gaps when certain sound elements are missing from an utterance (phoneme restoration).

3. What is the relation of cognitive psychology to cognitive science? Cognitive psychology is one of the constituent disciplines of cognitive science. Cognitive psychology examines representations and processes through its characteristic interplay of theory and experimentation. The other cognitive sciences include artificial intelligence, linguistics, neuroscience, and those parts of philosophy concerned with the mind.

4. Can one characterize Pavlov as an associationist? Yes, Pavlov was an associationist. However, his version of associationism is cast within a different context from that of the philosophers or from Ebbinghaus for that matter. Conducting his research on animals, Pavlov used behavioral manifestations of associations rather than introspective reports.

5. What is the relation of psycholinguistics and neuroscience? Psycholinguists have an interest in the neural structures and neural processes that support our use of language. They have also begun to investigate neural correlates of language comprehension and production, including language dysfunctions (See Chapter 11 for a fuller treatment of this question.)

6. You didn't list psychoanalysis as an antecedent of cognitive psychology? Why not? This is a good question. Psychoanalysis has been concerned with mental processing as is cognitive psychology. According to Erdelyi (1985), psychoanalysts have anticipated several information processing concepts, for example, working memory (the conscious). A good source on the relation between contemporary cognitive psychology and psychoanalysis is Erdelyi's (1985) book "Psychoanalysis: Freud's Cognitive Psychology". However, there are also important differences, cognitive psychologists have developed formal models of cognitive processing seeking to evaluate them in experiments. Freud's approach is more speculative and has not lent itself to an experimental assessment.

CHAPTER 2

1. In my introductory psychology class I have heard about animal research indicating that it made no difference to learning performance which part of the brain was removed. What mattered was the amount of brain tissue that was removed. Can we conclude from this that there is no localization of function in the brain? The research that you describe was conducted by Karl Lashley. He trained rats to traverse a maze, lesioned diverse sections of the rats' brains, and found that only the relative size of the lesion, but not its location affected performance. He reasoned that memories are distributed across different regions of the brain each of which contribute equally to performance. Subsequent research has called Lashley's data and conclusion into question. The principle of distributed memories itself may nevertheless apply, except representations are assumed to be distributed over a well circumscribed relatively small section of the brain (see also Chapter 4).

2. What do you mean by the phrase "the hippocampus is the teacher of the cortex?" Churchland and Sejnowski coined this phrase. They made reference to the model of the hippocampus as an organ to transform fragile into relatively permanent memories. In other words, the hippocampus strengthens acquired information much like a teacher does.

3. According to speculations mentioned in Chapter 2, the frontal lobes house an executive that schedules cognitive operations including speech production and problem solving. What controls the executive? This is a good question for which there is no one answer. I use this question as an occasion to introduce cognitive models that assume no executive centers, for example, neural network models.

4. How does one link the PET scan activity with the exact structures in the brain? One can't see the structures of the brain in a PET scan or can one? PET scans are used by neuroscientists to detect processing activity in specific structures associated with a particular cognitive task, for example, listening comprehension. PET activity reflects increased blood flow in a specific brain region.

5. How long does long-term potentiation (LTP) last and what is the significance of LTP? Does the firing rate eventually go back to the base rate? Long-term potentiation may last up to several weeks after the initial high-frequency stimulation has been applied. LTP represents a long-term change in neural response attributable to experience, as is true in other learning situations. However, no correlation between LTP and any behavioral measure has been established.

6. Neurons are firing at a certain base rate. What exactly changes when the firing rate increases? The permeability of the neuron membrane changes resulting in a chain of events at the level of ions. The net result is a brief depolarization. (For a detailed account see Carlson, 1991).

7. What can cognitive psychologists learn from clinical case studies about mental processes? Clinical cases suggest to researchers neural structures implicated in cognitive functioning in "normal" individuals. For example, the correlation between affluent aphasia, the lack of fluency in speech, and lesions in the left temporal lobe suggested to Broca that the temporal lobe is involved in speech production. (See also Chapter 11).

8. What is the difference between polarization and hyperpolarization? Polarization refers to the difference in polarity between the neuron and the membrane surface at rest. The soma is negative relative to the membrane surface. Hyperpolarization refers to the slight overshoot in negative polarity that follows an action potential, just before the resting potential is restored.

CHAPTER 3

1. Which neural site(s) is (are) impaired in individuals who exhibit blindsight? Such patients have suffered damage to the link between the lateral geniculate nucleus and nuclei in the V1 region of the visual cortex. As a result of this impairment, patients lose awareness of objects in certain locations but are nevertheless able to reach for the objects. (Consult the Weiskrantz source for further details. Also see Zeki, S. (1992). The visual image in mind and brain. *Scientific American*, 267, 43-50.).

2. Can attention enhance sensory activity in any sensory modality? According to Mangun and Hillyard's (1990) original hypothesis visual attention increases sensory activity in the visual pathways. The enhanced activity is reflected in increased ERP patterns. In subsequent research, the same authors have found that acoustic signals can also be enhanced through attention. It remains for future research to determine whether the enhancement hypothesis applies to other modalities.

3. What can we do to filter out unwanted stimuli? Many factors influence the success of filtering, for example, the salience of the primary and secondary stimuli, how much the primary task absorbs you, and what the payoffs for detecting the secondary stimuli are.

4. What are the neurological structures that support filtering? What does the continuum of automatic versus controlled processes have to do with Treisman's theory of feature integration? According to Treisman, detection is automatic, while integration is controlled.

5. What is the difference between the consistent and inconsistent conditions in the Schneider and Shiffrin (1977) experiment? In the consistent condition, targets and distractors are consistently assigned to different stimulus categories, for example letters versus numbers. In the inconsistent condition, the assignment of targets and distractors is inconsistent, for example, letters are used for targets as well as for distractors.

6. Is the ROC curve supposed to be the same for all 'normal' people? No, there are individual differences. The general shape however is as shown in Fig. 3.3.

7. How is it that someone can be carrying on a conversation with one person and still be able to comprehend and recognize what another person is saying? The shadowing research indicates that one doesn't recognize let alone comprehend much on the not-attended channel. To the extent that one does, the information pertains to the person. This indicates that information on the non-attended channel receives some degree of processing as proposed by the Deutsch-Norman model.

8. Can a person perform three or four, or even more tasks at the same time? In other words is there an upper limit to attention? The response to this question depends on one's theory. Classical theorists from James to Broadbent believed that a person can only focus on one task at a time.

More recently, theorists such as Schneider and Shiffrin have shown that performance on joint tasks improves as a function of practice. According to Spelke and colleagues, there is no upper limit, provided the person is willing to practice. The practical problem, however, is that hardly anyone is capable of devoting sufficient practice to doing three or more things at once.

CHAPTER 4

1. What is bottom-up information versus top-down information in pattern recognition? Bottom-up information refers to information associated with the stimulus, for example, the features of a letter. Top-down information refers to contextual information, for example, the word provides top-down information for a letter. A sentence provides top-down information for a word.

2. Is recognition of spoken words different for speakers of an ideographic language like Chinese? Auditory word recognition by definition must be based on acoustic features like formant position and transition.

3. What is the role of recognition mechanisms in 'projective' perception, for example, when someone thinks of a nebulous object like a cloud looking like a tree, train, or ship? This phenomenon illustrates the contribution of the observer (of top-down influences) on recognition. But remember the person still knows the cloud is not a tree! So recognition is codetermined by features of the stimulus itself.

4. The RBC theory suggests that we see objects in terms of their parts. How does this accord with the Gestalt view that we see objects as "wholes?" The apparent contradiction lies in the perspective one takes. Phenomenologically, we do see wholes, but from a processing point of view we recognize objects in terms of their components (see also Treisman theory in Ch. 3).

5. Explain why the Reicher (1969) experiment disconfirmed the guessing hypothesis? Because Reicher equated the level of chance performance (to 50% correct responses) in each of his three testing conditions.

6. What does the term population coding refer to and what does it have to do with reaching neurons? Your question is directed at research by Georgopoulo. He and his research team found neuron populations in the primary motor cortex of monkeys that become active when the animal moves its hand toward a specific direction. Other population of neurons respond when the animal makes a hand movement in a different direction. Population coding is the involvement of a given cell in movements of various directions and, conversely, a movement in a particular direction is associated with the activation of a population of cells.

7. My question concerns Fitts's Law. Why does width, W, appear in the denominator of the quotient on the right hand side? W appears in the denominator because of the inverse relation between response speed and width; your aiming response is faster the greater the wider the target is and it is slower as the target gets narrower.

8. Can you give another example for the degree-of-freedom principle in motor movements? The degrees of freedom of a motor response refer to the number of different ways in which you can make the response. For example, using your right hand you can turn a light switch in numerous

ways: you can lift your arm high above the switch, swing it up and down, left and right, circle around and finally aim at the switch to turn it; or you could first circle your arm, then move it diagonally, then make a circular motion, and then turn the switch. You can let your imagination run to invent other possible movements.

9. I have found that my performance in tennis diminishes after playing for longer than an hour. Does this not contradict the notion that practice improves performance? Performance in any given session of practice is determined by a variety of factors, including the player's overall level of practice (novice, intermediate, expert), the person's motivation and level of energy and fatigue. During a given game or practice session players will eventually get tired and play less well.

CHAPTER 5

1. Do people store different content information, for example, about plants and traffic signs in different locations in the brain? Your question is based on neuropsychological studies of two brain-damaged patients who exhibited a dissociation in the category naming task. For one of the patients, it was easier to processes names of animals than of man made objects, the other patient exhibited the reverse pattern. Intriguing as these results are, we must be cautious in generalizing to other individuals, because there were only two cases in the study and by definition their processing was impaired. It is nevertheless important to publish findings such as these so as to invite other researchers to confirm or disconfirm the results.

2. Is there any other way to achieve the autonomous stage than practice? According to cognitive psychologists, practicing a skill is the only way of insuring competence in it. So cognitive psychologists agree with the dictum that practice makes perfect. (Note, however, there is a debate in the literature on nativist issues of intelligence; see also Chapter 14).

3. Are there production rules telling a person what not to do in a particular situation? Production rules can elicit any sort of action, including not to do something.

4. Could instincts be considered a kind of innate knowledge or do they represent something else? One could classify instincts as a special kind of knowledge. Remember, however, they are not acquired as a result of learning. In any case, humans don't have many instincts, unlike birds and fish.

5. What is the difference between concepts, propositions, and production rules? Aren't they all rules? What is the distinction? A proposition represents an ordered set of concepts of the following format : Relation followed by one or more arguments. By contrast, a production rule consists of conditions and actions. The conditions specify the circumstances under which a certain action is invoked. According to Chapter 5, concepts embody knowledge of objects and events. Concepts may also be expressed as production rules, for example, one can identify a triangle by the following rule: "If the object has three interconnected sides then call it a triangle." In fact, according to theories of skill acquisition, concepts are converted into production rules through practice. The advantage is that production rules can be retrieved quickly.

6. I'm a little confused about production rules, perhaps because it seems too simplistic that every act should be the result of an "if-then" rule? What about all the complicated choices we have

to make? A complex skill like addition is based on many component skills involving many different rules. Similarly, according to production system theories, the choices we make are based on a set of many production rules, possibly counting in the thousands.

7. How did Ratcliff and McKoon determine from their experiment that people remember information in terms of propositions? The recognition latencies in their experiment were predicted by the propositional structure of the test sentences.

CHAPTER 6

Chapter 6 treats representation, retrieval, and learning in neural networks. Each of these is explained in terms of relatively simple mathematical notations and operations. A minority of students will find the calculations difficult. One can check students' understanding of equations and tables by having them do some calculations during class time. Some students tend to be unclear about the relation of the sample networks and illustrative calculations to cognition. For example, they ask for explanations for the initial choices for weights and input patterns selected in the chapter. The instructor is likely to hear such questions as "What do the input values represent? What do negative weights mean? What does the math of the connectionist networks have to do with psychology?" General comments such as the following surface as well: "Is psychology as mathematical as this class has been or is this just your approach?" and "I had no idea that this is what cognitive psychology is all about; in my other courses, I have only heard about the development of personality, the ego, id, and superego." Chapter 6 prompts the instructor to choose between treating quantitative models or not. I decided to cover them, although I found resistance among some students. Given this approach, I have found that detailed explanations of apparently simple concepts, for example matrix addition, are necessary. Of course, instructors will differ in their approaches, and the discussion of Chapter 6 may be adapted accordingly.

Specific questions:

1. I understand that one network can accommodate two (or more) separate input-output patterns, for example, roses, steaks etc. However what makes the network differentiate between the different inputs? How come each input pattern recreates its appropriate output? It is the combination of input activations AND the connection weights that produce the correct output.

2. Why do we discuss Hebbian learning if Delta learning is not only better but can also learn uncorrelated patterns as well?

3. Why are there new inputs for every trial in the Hebbian learning table (Table 6.5)? Using different patterns for the same network illustrates the principle of distributed representation of information. It also exemplifies the fact that learners may acquire a set of patterns rather than just one pattern.

4. I don't understand how the weights in a network relate to the nodes? The weights are a property of the links between nodes. The greater the weight the stronger is the link connecting two nodes.

5. How exactly does the Delta rule use feedback? It calculates the difference between actual and target outputs. By contrast, the Hebb rule pays no attention to that difference.

6. Can the Delta rule be used to account for learning of skills other than linguistic skills? Yes, the Delta rule is independent of particular skills. It can be used to acquire discriminations in pattern recognition, concept learning, motor learning, and other skills.

7. Is there any limit to learning by the Delta rule? Yes, there is. The rule cannot acquire the XOR-type patterns in Table 6.10.

8. Where do the original weights come from in the examples we've studied in the section on learning? They were 0 in each of our examples. This reflects typical practice in the literature. An alternative approach is to use random values as initial weights.

9. What is the significance of backpropagation learning? It overcomes limits of Delta learning with XOR type patterns.

10. What is the significance of backpropagation learning? Backpropagation learning is significant because it enables networks to acquire patterns that are not linearly separable. The XOR pattern in Table 6.10 illustrates such patterns. In general, backpropagation is required when different stimuli must be mapped into functionally similar responses. For example, there are different types of student performance that can earn a grade of A. Backpropagation learning is the most widely used of the learning procedures discussed in Chapter 6.

11. According to Elman (1993) working memory (WM) limitations are advantageous for a child learning syntactic structures. Why should this be true? Would it not be easier to acquire knowledge when the capacity of working memory is large? Elman (1993) made reference to a stage of language acquisition in children. During this stage, the children lack certain knowledge structures, for example, that sentences may exhibit long-distance dependencies between phrases (as in sentences with relative clauses). If the child had a large WM capacity she would remember all the phrases without being able to connect them. A small WM capacity, however, is just sufficient to support understanding of short and simple sentences and thus enable the child to learn their structure before learning more complex structures.

12. Would a four-layer network have fewer errors than a three-layer network or would the differences be minimal? Differences would be minimal. Consequently, theorists prefer three-layer networks. They are more parsimonious than and can achieve similar outcomes as more complex architectures.

13. Is there a way to determine high and low activation? These terms are relative. In our examples, -1 represents the highest level of inhibitory activation, 1 the highest level of excitatory activation, and 0 represents no activation.

14. Why do children learn irregular verbs before regular verbs? Because irregular verbs, although small in number, tend to occur more frequently in English and they are the ones a child encounters first.

15. What do you mean when you say that neural networks acquire their knowledge without programmer intervention? Doesn't the programmer have to construct the network and choose its parameters? The programmer selects the network architecture, chooses the parameters of learning, and figures out how to represent input and output in the given domain. However, the programmer does not have to represent every detail of the application as is true in the expert systems that have been developed within the symbol processing framework. Such expert systems are constructed by specially trained knowledge engineers who first interview experts in the domain and then express the components of knowledge in terms of hundreds of rules. The work of knowledge engineers becomes obsolete in neural networks.

CHAPTER 7

1. What is the significance of the learning rate in the Rescorla and Wagner (1972) rule (7.2)? The learning rate lr determines the speed with which the associative strength between the CS and the US approaches its theoretical maximum. The smaller lr is the smaller any changes in associative strength will be on any learning trial and the longer it will take to reach the maximum associative strength.

2. Does rehearsal affect short-term memory or long-term memory? According to the two-store model, rehearsal affects both stores: it maintains information in short-term memory and transfers it to long-term memory.

3. Don't subjects form associations among the items of a list to be studied for free recall? Would this not influence the shape of the serial position curve? Yes, they do. However, when results are averaged over trials and subjects, the U-shaped curve emerges.

4. Does the Bjork and Whitten study invalidate the results of the Glanzer and Cunitz experiment? No, it doesn't. It does, however, limit the generality of those results.

5. How do the critics of the two-store model of memory account for what happened in the case study of H.M.? One could conclude that you can't draw inferences from clinical case studies about memory processes in non-patient ("normal") individuals.

6. Do we remember information presented in different modalities for different lengths of time? In other words, which modality produces the best retention? This depends on the system of interest, the sensory register, short-term memory or long-term memory. At the level of the sensory register, it has been estimated that visual information is maintained for 1 sec while acoustic information is maintained for up to 4 sec. At other levels the response is less clear cut, because information presented in a specific modality is assumed to be transformed into a more abstract code.

7. Are there studies to show whether gender and age influence short-term memory? Men and women do not differ in short-term memory capacity, although some writers have suggested that there may be differences in access speed (e.g., Halpern, 1992, "Sex differences in cognitive abilities." Hillsdale, N.J.: Erlbaum). There is also a debate about the effects of age on working memory, and on memory in general. Light & Anderson (1985; Journal of Gerontology) have suggested that there are age related decrements in the memory span, while others view any

differences as minor (e.g., Rebok, G. W., 1985, Life-span cognitive development. New York: Holt). For a review of age differences and other memory systems see Mitchell (1985) Journal of Experimental Psychology: Learning, Memory, and Cognition, 15, 31 - 49.

8. According to Bartlett, where do the schemas come from that listeners use to interpret and remember stories? Schemas are acquired through experience in a particular context and environment. Schemas differ according to the social group and culture in which an individual grew up. Bartlett was specifically interested in such social and cultural differences and conducted some of his experiments among Swazi tribesmen in South Africa (Bartlett, 1932).

CHAPTER 8

1. Do we know how may subgoals are too many in the Tower of Hanoi problem or in any other problem for that matter? There is no absolute limit; it depends on the amount of practice a person has with a given task. A good estimate for novices is the generally assumed working memory capacity of 7 plus or minus 2 subgoals.

2. How do the results in Figure 8.8B support the idea of an exhaustive search? The slopes for yes- and no-responses do not differ. Because no-responses are necessarily based on an exhaustive search process, so must be the yes-responses.

3. Were there serial position effects in Sternberg's visual search task? That is, was 4 responded to faster in 4 2 3 6 than in 6 7 1 4? The typical result in the item-recognition study is that no such serial position effects occur. If they do occur at all this is due to unusual presentation conditions, for example, when the to-be-memorized set of digits is presented very rapidly.

4. Do we use exhaustive search methods only in experiments? When would we use a self-terminating search? According to Sternberg's theory, exhaustive search is a property of memory searches such as occur in the item-recognition task. Of course, Sternberg would not dispute that we use self-terminating searches, for example, when we look for objects in the real world.

5. Is there proof for the central executive in working memory? No, there is no proof. The central executive is an assumption of Baddeley's memory model. There are theorists, for example neural network theorists, who dispute its validity.

6. Does WM actually do the recognizing in the ACT system or does it take place in the entire information processing system? The latter is the case. Working memory, however, does play a central role. It is the processor that triggers specific productions when their conditions are matched to environmental events or to interim goals.

7. What is the difference between working memory and long-term memory? Working memory is the most active part of LTM.

8. Did SF's acquired memory skill show up in his course work, or did he just acquire a trick? SF's memory skill was limited for the domain that he trained in, the digit span. To the extent that SF practiced this skill he became an expert at memorizing digits. This is no different from

acquiring expertise in other domains, although the amount of training for most content domains, whether chess, medicine, or composing, will be more arduous and take longer.

9. Why should working memory be domain specific? Aren't there individuals who just remember any information better than others? This is an interesting question debated by researchers as discussed in Box 8.1. Note the synthesis proposed by Ericsson and Kintsch (1995). According to their view, there are two types of WM, LT-WM and ST-WM. The former is domain specific, while the latter is general.

CHAPTER 9

1. How did you arrive at the criterion value c=.40 used in Table 9.4? This is an arbitrary value intended to illustrate the threshold principle that underlies the criterion.

2. What, if any, are the differences between retrieval structure in the SAM model and neural networks? The two approaches are different. The SAM model is not a network through which activation is passed. There are no units, connections, and weights. The items in the SAM retrieval structure are mutually related, but their relation is abstract without connections. Unlike, connectionist networks, the SAM model is expressly a framework for retrieval. It does not purport to account for learning.

3. I was confused by the "fan effect." I'm not sure I understand how it could be harder to recall information when you know more about a concept. You put your finger on the "paradox of the expert." Remember that the concepts learned by Anderson's (1974) subjects were unrelated and selected arbitrarily. The facts predicated of doctor, sailor, hippie, and so on were selected randomly. In addition, subjects were asked to memorize the facts and to retrieve them verbatim. On the other hand, if subjects are asked to indicate whether or not certain facts are plausible, no fan effect or even a negative fan effect occurs (see Reder, 1987).

4. What is physically important to memory besides thiamine? Is there a memory drug? There is no known memory drug, there is no known substitute for memorization, elaboration, and attention at encoding.

5. What effect does autism have on memory? Why can autistic people remember such specific things that we can't?

6. Can chemically altered states affect learning and memory retrieval in the same way context or mood do? Yes, these are instances of state-dependent encoding. The typical finding is that information is better recalled if the retrieval context is similar to the encoding context. For example, individuals who consumed a specific drug during learning tend to recall more of the target information when they consume the same drug during testing (e.g., Eich, Weingartner, Stilliman, & Gillin, 1975, Journal of Verbal Learning and Verbal Behavior, 14, 408-417).

7. Does the part-list-cuing effect have any implications for the writing of exams, that is, would student performance be worse if the questions were to use exact wording from the text? One cannot answer this question without doing an experiment. You would need to write two versions of

the test, one including the verbatim quotes and the other version including paraphrases and compare student performance for both versions.

8. Do you think that neural activation is the same for real memories and for illusory memories? Could there some day be a cognitive lie-detector? The psychologist Daniel Schacter has measured PET activity in the illusory memory condition and in control conditions and found that there were both overlapping PET activity and PET activity unique to the nonillusory control condition. The overlapping PET activity for accurate and false memory items occurred in the hippocampus region. The true memory, however, also activated the left parietal region. This region is assumed to deal with sound patterns. It is too early to expect a cognitive lie-detector; remember that Schacter investigated memory for individual words tested a few minutes after the word list was presented. To assess more complex memories and long-term memories poses still greater challenges.

CHAPTER 10

1. How does linguistics help us in real life? How are linguistic rules applied? Theoretical linguists and applied linguists pursue different goals. They former seek to understand the structure of language in its own right, and by studying language they want to illuminate how the human mind works. It is the goal of applied linguists to use the discoveries of theoretical linguists in an applied context, for example, in second-language instruction.

2. Some of the syntactic rules we read about remind me of the rules we studied in elementary and high school. What is the difference between linguistic rules and those we learned in school? Linguists seek to discover the set of rules that generates all well-formed sentences of a language. They have uncovered rules far more subtle than those you've learned in schools. For example, consider examples (10.7) and (10.8) and see if you've acquired the information in school that is necessary to understand these sentences. The rules we learn in schools, by contrast, are instructions on how to form the most typical types of sentences in a language, for example, active sentences, passive sentences, questions, and commands. These rules are not intended as formal descriptions of a language.

3. What do you mean by the sentence "A rule is defined as recursive if it *calls* itself"?
Consider an example from Box 10.1, the definition of factorials. The definition of a factorial is given by expressions (1) and (2)

(1) $n! = n \times (n-1)!$
(2) $0! = 1$

Expression (1) is a recursive expression because the factorial on the left side is calculated in terms of the factorial on the right side. We say $n!$ *calls* $(n-1)!$

4. According to Chapter 10, words may be broken down into other words. For example, "kill" may be interpreted as "becoming not alive." How far can one go with these analyses and when you get to the primitives, what are they? Linguists and computational linguists have addressed this issue of "meaning primitives." Schank, for example, arrived at a relatively small number of meaning primitives that underlie verbs. Two of these are TRANS and ATRANS. TRANS represents the notion of physical transfer in such verbs as to bring, to send, to carry, and to lift.

ATRANS refers to transfer of abstract entities as implied in such verbs as to sell, to buy, to exchange, and to give.

5. Explain the difference between the transformational approach and the principle-based approach to grammar. According to transformational grammar, sentences are generated via phrase-structure rules and transformational rules as illustrated in Figures 10.4 and 10.5. In short, the transformational approach is based on explicit rewrite rules. The principle-based framework, however, invokes a sequence of principles rather than of rules. The principle-based approach to parsing is treated in Berwick (1991).

6. Give an example of a sentence generated according to principles rather than phrase structure and transformational rules. Both approaches produce the same sentences, although the route they take is different.

7. I'm interested in knowing just how old Chomsky and his students were when they developed their theories? They were relatively young. Chomsky was in his mid-twenties when he worked on phrase structure rules and 28 when they were published in 1956. He began work on transformational grammar soon thereafter.

CHAPTER 11

1. How does the claim that there are no forward inferences accord with Zola's finding of facilitation for phrases like "buttered popcorn" as opposed to adequate popcorn? Modular theorists attribute such context effects to post-access integration rather than to a forward looking expectation. In other words, the facilitation of "buttered popcorn" occurs because "popcorn" is more easily integrated with "buttered" than with "adequate."

2. Chapter 11 dealt primarily with written language comprehension. Are there different processes in the comprehension of spoken language? The response to your question is yes and no. On the one hand, there are differences at the encoding stage: the speech signal is different from the written input (see Chapter 4). In addition, there are patterns of pauses and emphases in speech that provide clues to the listener about sentence structure and meaning. On the other hand, psycholinguists assume that language input, whether spoken or written, is transformed into an abstract format, for example, into propositions. At this stage, the same comprehension processes are assumed to operate.

3. Why does the neighborhood effect support the interactive comprehension model rather than the modular model? According to interactive models, there should be facilitated word identification among similar words because they share overlapping features. The search model predicts that a word with many neighbors should take longer to recognize because the search has to cover more items. The data confirm the prediction of the interactive model: recognition was faster the more neighbors a word has.

4. Is listening comprehension easier than reading comprehension or vice versa? As infants we first master listening comprehension. We do so quite naturally without formal instruction. Most of us learn reading only once we enter school (see also Chapter 15). At these early stages, listening is easier than reading. However for mature readers the difference is less, indeed the reverse may

be true. In general, the facility of reading comprehension depends on the amount of reading a person does.

5. What good does creating computers do that generate and comprehend sentences, except that lonely people will be able to talk to them? There are good theoretical and practical reasons to program computers to understand and produce language. Programs that simulate language processing advance theory development and research in psycholinguistics. As for practical reasons, computational linguists are interested in speech understanding, translation, summarization, and question-answering programs. Each of these is useful for specific purposes, for example, for banking transactions, information entry into and retrieval from data bases, and for abstracting lengthy documents.

6. What can we learn from computational linguists about human language comprehension? Can one say that the computer rules of the program are the same that humans use? That depends on the goal of the program developer. Some programs, for example, CAPS were intended as simulations of human language understanding. Others are designed to get a specific job done, regardless of human processing considerations.

CHAPTER 12

1. How do propositions 1 - 6 in Figure 12.3 represent a cycle in Kintsch and van Dijk's model? Kintsch and van Dijk (e.g., 1978) assumed that readers must process a text in terms of segments because of working memory limitations. They also suggested that readers use clause and sentence boundaries as convenient demarcations of text segments or cycles. The first sentence in Figure 12.3 constitutes a cycle of six propositions, a number well within the widely accepted limit of seven plus or minus two chunks of working memory.

2. What is the difference between backward and forward inferences? A backward inference is necessary to integrate sentences that appear to lack coherence as example 12.10 illustrates. A forward inference expresses an expectation of subsequent events or elaborates the information in a given sentence. For example, the implied instrument of sweeping, "broom," represents a forward inference implicit in "John swept the floor."

3. Can one use the difference in visual lateral masking between dyslexic and normal readers to train dyslexic readers to read like normals? In other words, is there a way of training dyslexics to exhibit the same masking patterns as do normals? Your question makes reference to research by Geiger and colleagues (1994). Their research team found that in normal readers visual lateral masking is greater in the periphery of the visual field with best letter and word identification in the center of the gaze. Lateral masking in dyslexic readers is greatest in the center. Using a moving window technique, Geiger and his team trained dyslexic children to read so that visual masking was similar to that of normal readers. The dyslexic children did improve their reading level. However, the benefit was relatively small. Consider also that the number of subjects was less than 30 and that dyslexia may stem from a wide variety of etiologies. Nevertheless, your question points in the right direction: rehabilitation can begin once researchers have identified specific processing differences between patients and nonpatients.

4. What is your advice on how to finish the term paper most efficiently? Although I have assigned term papers and given advice to paper writers many times I find it difficult to give you a "cookbook" answer on paper writing because students and circumstances tend to differ. Nevertheless, since you asked the question, here are a couple of suggestions that I have found helpful. (1) You can only write about something when you have knowledge about the topic. My first suggestion, therefore, is to do research on the topic; generally the more research you do the better. As you do your research, take notes, formulate questions, and identify patterns in the data or theories. (2) Use your notes to organize ideas for a draft paper. At this stage, do not worry about the final version of the paper. Try to concentrate on developing ideas. When you are ready to draft the paper, try to write whatever your mood. Don't wait until you are in the "right mood." (3) Write drafts, reread them, and improve them as you go along. Set a personal deadline or a maximum number of drafts so that you finish on time and don't work on your paper in perpetuity. - I offer no guarantees that these suggestions are efficient but I have found that they have helped students to complete their term papers on time.

CHAPTER 13

1. Is a genius generally smart? Can he or she solve problems in many different domains? We'll explore creativity and genius in Chapter 14. According to some scholars, for example, Galton, genius is hereditary. Cognitive psychologists such as Ericsson and collegues attribute creative acts and problem solving ability to extended practice within a particular domain. (see Ericsson, Krampe, & Tesch-Roemer, 1993, Psychological Review, 100, 363-406.)

2. Does knowledge-rich problem solving include both procedural and declarative knowledge? What is the relation between fact retrieval and solving knowledge-rich problems? Problem solving depends on procedural and declarative knowledge and both of these types of knowledge include factual information. As a result, solving knowledge-rich problems does involve fact retrieval. Facts may be retrieved by various routes; they may be represented as production rules or as propositions (see also Chapter 5).

3. How would the Table Search Model account for subtraction? Does subtraction take longer than addition? Is subtraction more difficult the greater the terms? In order to handle subtraction problems, one dimension of the table would represent the minuend and the other the subtrahend. The results could be arranged in matrix form as in Figure 13.8 A. Assuming that beginning students are not yet familiar with negative numbers, results of less than 0 may have to be excluded. In any case, note that the Table Search Model has been superseded by other models like the Direct Association model. There is no reason why subtraction and addition problems should differ in execution time. The variable that affects execution time in the direct association model is the occurrence frequency of the problem for the particular person.

4. Have there been studies analyzing gender differences in the verbal part of the SAT (like Linne & Hyde did for the quantitative part)? Hyde and Linne (1988) conducted a large-scale review of gender differences in verbal ability and published their results in Psychological Bulletin, 104, 53-69. They found a very slight advantage for verbal ability in females under 5 years and over 26 years of age. Hyde and Linne emphasize the fact that the differences were very small. (For a different perspective see Sex Differences in Cognitive Abilities by Diane Halpern, 1992, Erlbaum Publishers.)

5. How does Anderson's et al. (1984) Lisp tutor internalize a student's cognitive processes? The LISP tutor is based on production rules. Some of these are designed to detect learners' response patterns, including errors. Using such response patterns the system "infers" the productions (or processes) that must have produced them. This rationale is analogous to attributing the faulty reasoning in arithmetic to specific procedures (see Box 5.1)

CHAPTER 14

1. Explain the number series 72, 43, 90, 71, 47, 85, 70, 51, 80 given at the beginning of the chapter. What do the terms (-1, +4, -5) refer to? What is the next number in the sequence and why? This number series consists of successive sets of three numbers each of which is changed by a different magnitude: one subtracts 1 from the first number, one adds 4 to the second number, and one subtracts 5 from the third number. As a result, the next set of three numbers consists of 69, 55, and 75.

2. Define recursion and give an everyday example for recursion. Why is recursion so important? Why do I find it difficult to understand? The philosopher Douglas Hofstaedter (1979) has a good treatment of recursion in his book "Goedel, Escher, Bach." He lists several examples of recursion: stories inside stories, movies inside movies, paintings inside paintings, and Russian dolls inside Russian dolls. He describes a recursive definition as a definition in which something is being defined in terms of a simpler version of itself (see examples in Box 10.1). Finally Hofstaedter offers an everyday example by noting that recursion occurs "when you postpone completing a task in favor of a simpler task" (pg. 127). Suppose the following scenario: a friend (A) is calling you on the phone asking you a question that you can't answer. Using the hold facilities of your fancy phone, you keep A on hold, and call somebody else (B) who you think does know the answer. Further assume B doesn't know the answer either, but tells you to call C, but be sure to inform him, B, as well. So you call C; assume you receive the answer, you stop talking to C and resume the conversation with B who has been on hold. Finally you resume the conversation with A and tell him the answer. This example illustrates the idea that the top goal is achieved by pushing the solution effort to different levels. Once the problem is solved at a given level, attention pops back to the prior level. Recursive thinking is difficult because one has to devise a solution plan and remember a variety of subgoals.

3. I don't understand the use of the connectionist model in the Gluck and Bower experiment. First of all, how do the connectionist network predictions differ from those based on Bayes' theorem? The network calculates its predictions according to the delta rule, while the predictions from Bayes' theorem are illustrated in expression (1) in Chapter 14.

4. Are the network's predictions based on the choice of inputs or the manipulation of the symptoms? The network predictions result from the delta learning rule; this rule uses inputs and adjusts connection weights so as to generate output that approximates the target output. However, in the Gluck and Bower study, the delta rule produced a non-optimal outcome. It thus mimicked the performance of the human learners. The students and the network fell prey to the representativeness fallacy. Neither considered the small overall frequency of rarities in the population as a whole.

5. Is there any evidence that people acquire concepts unconsciously? Most of the concepts that we use in everyday life were acquired without awareness. People use the word representing the concept in different contexts again and again and thus acquire the concept. This is an implicit learning situation. Reber (1993) has captured implicit learning situations in a grammar learning task. He constructed artificial grammars based on a set of transition rules and on letter strings. Some of the letter strings were formed in accordance with specific rules of the grammar; other strings were not. Without being told the difference, subjects had an easier time learning the rule-based strings than random strings.

6. Which is the correct prediction in the Gluck and Bower (1988) study, the prediction from Bayes' theorem or the neural network prediction? From a medical point of view, the prediction derived from Bayes' theorem is the correct prediction. In the psychology experiment, performance of subjects was predicted more successfully by the neural network prediction. Remember though that subject performance was in error! So in this case your best bet is Bayes' theorem.

CHAPTER 15

1. Why aren't there more applications of Cognitive Psychology in every-day life? There are at least two responses possible to this question. First, principles of cognitive psychology yet to be discovered have probably already been applied. Consider the example of the therapist who developed an instructional reading system for a dyslexic patient without knowing formal theories of reading. Second, in his assessment of the future of cognitive engineering, Landauer mentions several reasons why cognitive psychology has not been applied to a greater extent: Cognitive psychologists usually study abstract mental processes rather than specific applications. Design engineers used to have relatively little knowledge of the models proposed by cognitive researchers. Finally, many of the findings in cognitive psychology are relatively small, but for practical applications one needs to investigate large and robust effects. Nevertheless, Landauer feels that an expansion of present knowledge in cognitive research will eventually lead to its application in the workplace.

2. Explain the performance operating characteristic (POC) and show how it might be used in applied settings. The POC measures a person's performance on two tasks. Three kinds of measurements are taken, namely one on task 1, one on task 2, and finally a measurement is taken on both tasks executed jointly. Performance on each task is plotted along a separate axis. Performance usually drops when a person performs the two responses at the same time. The POC paradigm is used in laboratory simulations rather than in real-life situations.

3. You said that according to research results, there is no advantage of an alphabetic arrangement of type writer keys. Based on a person's extended practice with the alphabet I would have expected the alphabetic arrangement to work best. Can you explain this result again? It is apparently relatively easy for subjects to learn any letter sequence so that there is a minimal advantage of the alphabet if there is one at all. The advantage of practice accrues to skills more complex than letter sequences. Also remember that learning the letter sequence is only one of the component skills of typing.

4. Were there any gender differences in Klahr and Carver's study of Logo learning and transfer? I found no mention of gender differences in Klahr and Carver's (1988) report. Note, however, that their study sought to shed light on the transfer issue rather than on gender differences.

5. Are there are methods of teaching reading other than the phonics and the whole-word method? These two methods are prototypical; there are a variety of descendants of these methods. For further details see Adams (1990) "Beginning to read: thinking and learning about print."

6. My question concerns prospective memory. The text defines prospective memory as memory to execute specific tasks at some future point. I don't see how this differs from other types of memory because in each case you must remember some information that was given to you in the past. Could you explain? You are right when you state that memory tasks require memory for information acquired in the past. This does include instructions to carry out a future act. The aspect in which prospective memory differs from retrospective memory is that the person must also remember the trigger to elicit the response at some point in the future. Conceptual issues on prospective memory are discussed in the following book: Bradimonte, M., Einstein, G.O., and McDaniel (1996). Prospective memory: theory and applications. Mahwah, NJ: Erlbaum.

MULTIPLE CHOICE QUESTIONS

CHAPTER 1

(a) 1. The following description describes the philosopher Descartes most accurately

    (a) he introduced the idea of specific mental objects and structures
    (b) he emphasized the primacy of sensory experience over reason
    (c) he considered response speed as a reflection of reasoning processes
    (d) he inspired anatomical and physiological investigation of the brain

(c) 2. David Hume's philosophy may be described as

    (a) rationalist
    (b) analytical
    (c) empiricist
    (d) existential

(c) 3. According to historians, the first experimental psychologist was

    (a) W. James
    (b) I. Pavlov
    (c) W. Wundt
    (d) G. Fechner

(a) 4. The difference threshold is best described as

    (a) the ratio of the perceived difference to the standard stimulus iconstant
    (b) the threshold at different levels of the stimulus scale is constant
    (c) the ratio of the standard stimulus to the comparison stimulus is constant
    (d) the ratio of the standard stimulus to the comparison stimulus is variable

(b) 5. It was the principal goal of introspectionists to uncover

    (a) mental processes
    (b) mental structures
    (c) attention processes
    (d) personal experiences

(d) 6. The subtraction method was used by

    (a) researchers studying animal behavior
    (b) introspectionists comparing two different perceptual experiences
    (c) psychophysicists examining the difference threshold
    (d) experimenters studying the duration of mental operations

(d) 7. The French philosopher Descartes introduced the idea of mental structures. The contemporary term for these structures is

  (a) abstract ideas
  (b) veridical image
  (c) mental models
  (d) mental representations

(d) 8. The idea of "mental representation" is fundamental to cognitive psychology and cognitive science. Please choose the set of attributes that best characterizes mental representations. They are

  (a) abstract, conscious, spatial
  (b) abstract, overt, neural
  (c) conscious, neural, spatial
  (d) abstract, symbolic, manipulable

(a) 9. According to Kant, a category is

  (a) an abstract characterization of the relations among objects
  (b) a class of objects, for example, of furniture, animals, or plants
  (c) a generic concept used to describe general properties of objects
  (d) an innate dimension that our mind uses to perceive objects

(b) 10. Psychophysicists examined the relation between

  (a) a standard and a comparison stimulus
  (b) psychological experience and changes in a stimulus continuum
  (c) the absolute threshold and the difference threshold
  (d) a physical continuum and the observable behavior of subjects

(d) 11. Wundt considered psychology as the "science of experience." He proposed three different states of experience. They are

  (a) sensations, representations, images
  (b) thoughts, images, reactions
  (c) emotions, thoughts, memories
  (d) sensations, images, feelings

(c) 12. Introspectionism was a method used by such pioneers of psychology as Wundt and James. Which of the following is an appropriate characterization of introspectionism?

  (a) it was successful in discovering the elements of the human mind.
  (b) it was not successful in discovering the elements of the human mind.
  (c) it was based on subjective reports and therefore challenged by the behaviorists.
  (d) it lead to important insights on the effect of attention on sensation and perception.

(a) 13. The first psychologist to examine memory in experiments was

- (a) Ebbinghaus
- (b) Donders
- (c) Wundt
- (d) Helmholtz

(c) 14. Ebbinghaus used the following methods in his experimental study of memory.

- (a) introspective method, anticipation method
- (b) associative method, psychophysical method
- (c) anticipation method, paired-associate method
- (d) subtraction method, paired-associate method

(d) 15. According to behaviorists, learning is

- (a) the acquisition of knowledge as a result of reinforcement
- (b) the acquisition of new responses resulting from practice
- (c) the change in behavior resulting from reinforcement
- (d) the change in behavior resulting from practice

(a) 16. The Gestalt psychologists were contemporaries of behaviorist researchers. Choose the most fitting description of Gestalt psychology from among the following.

- (a) they investigated perceptual phenomena
- (b) they investigated perceptual and stimulus generalization
- (c) they resurrected the introspective method
- (d) they proposed mental representations to explain Gestalt principles.

(c) 17. Helmholtz developed the subtraction method to investigate

- (a) the detection time in choice experiments
- (b) the difference threshold in psychophysical experiments
- (c) the speed of neural transmission
- (d) the reaction time of subjects in signal detection tasks

(a) 18. In choice experiments, reaction times change as a function of the number of choices the subject must make. The following expression describes the relation between number of choices and reaction times

- (a) reaction times increase by a constant with the doubling of the number of alternatives
- (b) reaction times increase exponentially as the number of alternatives increases
- (c) reaction times increase with the doubling of the alternatives up to eight alternatives
- (d) reaction times increase with the number of choices and reach an asymptote after 7 alternatives.

(c) 19. Identify the statement that best describes the goal of linguistic research according to Noam Chomsky.

    (a) discover the mental processes we use to understand and produce language
    (b) compare the evolution of syntactic patterns in different languages and arrive at a set of principles common to all languages
    (c) discover rules used to generate grammatical sentences in a language
    (d) use the expressions of language to deduce the processes and structure of the mind

(d) 20. The introduction of computers contributed to the emergence of cognitive psychology because

    (a) the computer has memory stores whose functions reflect properties of human memory
    (b) computers have stimulated research in human learning and memory
    (c) the logic of computer programs reflects the sequence of mental processes
    (d) the architecture of the computer provides a metaphor for the human mind

(b) 21. The functionalist approach to cognition

    (a) emphasizes the biological functions that underlie our mental operations
    (b) suggests that the study of cognitive and neural processes is independent
    (c) proposed that mental functions exert an influence on neural and physiological processes
    (d) holds that one must examine experience and behavior as a function of mental structures and observable stimuli

(c) 22. The Atkinson and Shiffrin model of information processing includes the following major structures.

    (a) small-capacity store, long-term store, CPU
    (b) sensory register, symbolic processor, central executive
    (c) long-term store, sensory register, short-term store
    (d) central processor, input processors, output processors

(b) 23. Cognitive psychology is based on the two following basic ideas.

    (a) knowledge, structure
    (b) process, representation
    (c) process, behavior
    (d) theories, methods

(a) 24. The experiment is the primary research tool of cognitive psychologists because

    (a) it affords the potential of controlling extraneous factors
    (b) it provides the only objective means to assess mental processes
    (c) researchers can replicate experimental results
    (d) experiments are motivated by theories of cognition

(c) 25. The type of data preferred by cognitive psychologists are the following

   (a) phenomenological reports
   (b) neurophysiological responses
   (c) chronometric measures
   (d) percentage of correct responses

(d) 26. After witnessing a crime, what may cause a witness to give faulty evidence?

   (a) impressions are formed in a hurry
   (b) he/she tries to block the event from memory
   (c) the method of questioning
   (d) a & c

(c) 27. Which of the following was a rationalist?

   (a) Hume
   (b) Kant
   (c) Descartes
   (d) Pavlov

(a) 28. According to René Descartes the mind contains

   (a) structures
   (b) feature detectors
   (c) logical entities
   (d) schemas

(d) 29. According to David Hume, (1711-1776), our ideas are based on

   (a) memorable experiences
   (b) thoughts that are triggered through stimulation
   (c) internal sublimation
   (d) experience with the external world

(c) 30. Which of the following philosophers held that the mind without experience is empty and experience without the mind is blind?

   (a) Kant
   (b) Hume
   (c) Descartes
   (d) Aristotle

(c) 31. Immanuel Kant identified both the mind and experience as sources of knowledge. Experience provides the data, while the mind provides the structure of knowledge. According to Kant, the mental structures are

- (a) schemas, algorithms, dimensions
- (b) categories & dimensions, algorithms
- (c) categories & dimensions, schemas
- (d) none of the above

(d) 32. Psychophysicists such as Weber and Fechner reasoned that physical events in the environment give rise to

- (a) autonomic stimulation
- (b) emotions
- (c) accelerated heart rates
- (d) psychological sensations

(b) 33. Wundt defined psychology as the "science of experience." According to Wundt, the mind includes three basic states

- (a) complex feelings, images, sensations
- (b) simple feelings, images, sensations
- (c) nerve impulses, lexicon, sensations
- (d) working memory, lexicon, sensations

(c) 34. James wrote, "When two elementary brain-processes have been active together or in immediate succession, one of them, in re-occurring, tends to propagate its excitement into the other." What type of theory is best expressed by the quote above?

- (a) Behaviorism
- (b) Psychophysiology
- (c) Associationism
- (d) Neural psychology

(b) 35. Gestalt psychologists wanted to understand our

- (a) elemental sensations of configurations
- (b) perception of stimulus configurations
- (c) relational perception
- (d) associative responses

(c) 36. Pavlov was one of the first researchers to study learning. He introduced the Classical Conditioning paradigm. This paradigm

    (a) involves the presentation of a sound and meat to a dog
    (b) compares a subject's reaction to the conditioned stimulus with that to a neutral test stimulus
    (c) presents two unrelated stimuli in association
    (d) is used to study the digestive system in dogs and other organisms

(c) 37. The goal of human factors research was to

    (a) design equipment to be more efficient
    (b) design equipment to be based on the characteristics of the human operator without his limitations
    (c) design equipment on the characteristics of the human operator with his limitations
    (d) develop computerized equipment

(a) 38. Noam Chomsky studied the structure of language in its many forms. His approach could best be described as

    (a) rationalist
    (b) associationist
    (c) structuralist
    (d) introspectionist

(b) 39. Listening comprehension involves several stages: encoding the words, analyzing the sentences syntactically and linking the information across sentences. According to cognitive theories, these processes are

    (a) conscious
    (b) unconscious
    (c) innate
    (d) sequential

(d) 40. The functionalist view allows scientists to

    (a) study the differences between the human mind and computers
    (b) study the encoding processes of the human mind
    (c) study cognition as a function of biology
    (d) study cognition without having to study its biological basis

(c) 41. According to cognitive psychologists, knowledge is

    (a) abstract
    (b) specific
    (c) structured
    (d) innate

(a) 42. In an experiment, one systematically varies the _____ and studies the changes in the _____.

- (a) independent variable, dependent variable
- (b) dependent variable, independent variable
- (c) general variable, specific variable
- (d) specific variable, general variable

(b) 43. Confounding factors limit a researcher's ability to interpret the results of an experiment. A confounding variable

- (a) covaries with the dependent variable
- (b) covaries with the independent variable
- (c) limits the test-retest reliability
- (d) influences the retention of nonsense syllables

(d) 44. The computer model of Selfridge and Neisser was developed to stimulate visual letter recognition. The model

- (a) encodes the usual stimulus
- (b) detects the features of the letter
- (c) compares the description of the letters with templates stored in memory
- (d) includes all of the above

(b) 45. Kant introduced three major mental representations: dimensions, categories, and schemas. According to Kant, dimensions

- (a) accommodate the rotation of the object in space
- (b) represent the extension of the object in space and time
- (c) represent the field of vision that the object encompasses
- (d) represent the rate at which a moving object is seen in the subject's field of vision

(b) 46. A problem with the introspective method is that

- (a) it is difficult to identify a subject's thought processes
- (b) observations are too subjective to classify
- (c) it is too time consuming
- (d) all of the above

(d) 47. New adaptations of Donders' subtraction method use the PET scan to examine the brain under a load condition to asses metabolic activity. For comparison researchers would look at the:

- (a) response time
- (b) visual processing
- (c) stimulus intensity
- (d) baseline condition

(b) 48. The information-processing approach of making symbols, processes, and their sequence explicit, is illustrated visually by:

    (a) a spreadsheet
    (b) a flowchart
    (c) a diagram
    (d) a program

(d) 49. Conscious and unconscious states of cognition are still difficult to capture with current investigative methods. Research questions arise as to how to investigate the different states, and whether

    (a) the two states occur in parallel
    (b) the unconscious uses more processing space
    (c) there are different representations for the content of conscious and unconscious
    (d) (a) and (c)

(c) 50. Computer simulations of cognitive processes can discover unexpected results and relationships between the processes. However, a drawback is that model builders may be guided not by psychological theories, but by

    (a) too little knowledge of computers
    (b) dated ideas
    (c) programming considerations
    (d) artificial intelligence

CHAPTER 2

(a) 1. Both brain hemispheres consist of four lobes. Which of the four lobes is not involved in sensory processing?

    (a) frontal
    (b) parietal
    (c) temporal
    (d) occipital

(b) 2. Computer tomography (CT) scans are useful to analyze static brain structures. They are not as useful for studying cognitive processes because such processes

    (a) occur in regions of the brain not accessible to CT
    (b) occur in real time
    (c) can only be detected through X-rays
    (d) can not be detected by any form of electrophysiogical imaging

(c)   3.   In one condition of Posner's (1988) study of cognitive processes and metabolic rate of the brain, subjects were presented words over headphones. Using PET-scans, Posner found that blood flow increased _____ during this condition

   (a) in the occipital lobe but not in the parietal lobe
   (b) in auditory centers but not visual centers
   (c) in both the occipital and parietal lobes
   (d) in both auditory and visual centers

(a)   4.   Haier and his colleagues (1992) measured the brain activity in their subjects at various stages of learning to play the computer game TETRIS. Haier reported that brain activity _____ the more the subjects were exposed to the game.

   (a) decreased
   (b) increased
   (c) remained constant
   (d) was in a constant flux

(b)   5.   Brain waves are measured by placing electrodes on multiple sites on the skull. The pattern of brain wave activity obtained by averaging numerous brain wave patterns over many trials is termed the

   (a) magnetoencephalograph
   (b) event-related potential
   (c) convergence of evidence
   (d) electroencephalogram

(c)   6.   According to the standard view of early cognitive psychologists the following relation is true

   (a) cognitive psychology : software = computer science : hardware
   (b) computer simulation : experiments = computer science : computer programs
   (c) cognitive psychology : physiological psychology = computer science : electrical engineering
   (d) cognitive psychology : experimental psychology = software engineering : hardware engineering

(c)   7.   The neuron is the basic building block of the nervous system. Choose the statement that does NOT apply to neurons

   (a) the neuron is a communication station
   (b) neurons in different species exhibit the same basic anatomy
   (c) neurons are relatively uniform
   (d) neurons include a soma and projections

(d) 8. The cell body of a neuron contains the nucleus and tissue which supports the operation of the cell. It is known as the

- (a) glia
- (b) ganglion
- (c) stem
- (d) soma

(c) 9. The long projection of the neuron that transmits electrical impulses to terminal buttons is the

- (a) dendrite
- (b) myelin sheath
- (c) axon
- (d) neurotransmitter

(b) 10. Chemically coded information is transmitted from one neuron to neighboring neurons via the

- (a) dendrites
- (b) terminal buttons
- (c) axons
- (d) neurotransmitters

(a) 11. The neuron's projection that receives information from neighboring neurons is called

- (a) dendrite
- (b) terminal button
- (c) axon
- (d) neurotransmitter

(b) 12. Neurons have been described as communication stations. They communicate with

- (a) other neurons and with skeletal muscles
- (b) other neurons, muscles, and other organs
- (c) other neurons only
- (d) motor neurons and sensory neurons

(c) 13. When neurotransmitters travel across the synaptic cleft, the permeability of the postsynaptic membrane is changed in an excitatory or inhibitory manner. Inhibitory postsynaptic potential (IPSP) involves ____ at the postsynaptic membrane.

- (a) slight decrease in the positivity of the resting potential
- (b) a slight increase in the positivity of the resting potential
- (c) a slight decrease in the negativity of the resting potential
- (d) a slight increase in the negativity of the resting potential

(a) 14. The variety among the neurotransmitters matches that of the neural system they serve. Researches have identified many neurotrsansmitters and their known functions. Which of these neurotransmitters acts as an inhibitor at both the synaptic and behavioral levels?

- (a) Serotonin
- (b) Norepinephrine
- (c) Acetylcholine
- (d) Dopamine

(b) 15. The structure that provides an insulating envelope around neurons and axons is known as the

- (a) myelin sheath
- (b) glia cell
- (c) neuron membrane
- (d) synaptic membrane

(b) 16. The technique developed to investigate processing in neural pathways, in which a non-toxic radioactive substance is injected in specific structures and, using x-rays, their passage through the fibers is monitored, is called

- (a) event-related images
- (b) positron emission tomography
- (c) magnetic resonance imaging
- (d) computerized axial tomography

(c) 17. The communication of impulses based on electrophysiological and neurochemical processes is referred to as

- (a) neural polarization
- (b) neural projection
- (c) neural transmission
- (d) hyperpolarization

(a) 18. During a resting state the inside of the neuron is slightly negative relative to its outside. In this state the neuron is

- (a) polarized
- (b) depolarized
- (c) hyperpolarized
- (d) ionic

(b) 19. When the inside of a neuron is slightly positive relative to its outside it is

- (a) polarized
- (b) depolarized
- (c) hyperpolarized
- (d) ionic

(c) 20. There is a spike in the neuron's activity as a result of a brief electrical charge applied at rest. It lasts less than a millisecond and is referred to as

- (a) polarization
- (b) hyperpolarization
- (c) action potential
- (d) none of the above

(c) 21. Immediately after the action potential the negative potential overshoots the resting potential by a small amount. This state is known as

- (a) polarization
- (b) depolarization
- (c) hyperpolarization
- (d) ionic state

(d) 22. The messengers of neural impulses in the synaptic cleft are known as

- (a) neurons
- (b) sensory neurons
- (c) motor neurons
- (d) neurotransmitters

(c) 23. There are at least _____ known neurotransmitters.

- (a) 1000
- (b) 100
- (c) 50
- (d) 10

(b) 24. A neuron's response to stimulation is governed by the

- (a) law of effect
- (b) all-or-none law
- (c) state of activation
- (d) none of the above

(c) 25. The point beyond which a neuron responds at an activity level above its resting activity level is the

- (a) graded potential
- (b) excitation level
- (c) threshold
- (d) inhibition level

(a) 26. The varied level of output at the dendrite that changes in proportion with the intensity of the stimulus is the

    (a) graded potential
    (b) excitation level
    (c) threshold
    (d) inhibition level

(c) 27. The _____ of the neuron sends information across the synapse.

    (a) axon
    (b) dendrite
    (c) presynaptic membrane
    (d) postsynaptic membrane

(d) 28. The _____ of the neuron receives information from across the synapse.

    (a) axon
    (b) dendrite
    (c) presynaptic membrane
    (d) postsynaptic membrane

(c) 29. Depolarization of the receiving neuron corresponds to a state of

    (a) habituation
    (b) sensitization
    (c) excitation
    (d) inhibition

(c) 30. Select the neurotransmitter found in nerves that serve the skeletal muscles, heart, and autonomic nervous system. It has an excitatory effect on skeletal fibers and an inhibitory effect on cardiac fibers.

    (a) serotonin
    (b) norepinephrine
    (c) acetylcholine
    (d) gamma-aminobutyric acid

(b) 31. Identify the neurotransmitter that influences the degree of alertness in the brain. It acts as an inhibitor in the central nervous system, but has an excitatory effect in the autonomous nervous system.

    (a) serotonin
    (b) norepinephrine
    (c) acetylcholine
    (d) gamma-aminobutyric acid

(c) 32. The increase in response to a neutral stimulus if it is preceded by a painful and potentially noxious stimulus is best described by

(a) polarization
(b) excitation
(c) sensitization
(d) hyperpolarization

(b) 33. The loss of speech in patients whose speech comprehension remains intact is referred to as

(a) stroke
(b) aphasia
(c) amnesia
(d) alzheimer's

(d) 34. The _____ evolved from the spinal cord; it includes the medulla, the cerebellum, the limbic system, and the reticular formation.

(a) forebrain
(b) midbrain
(c) thalamus
(d) brainstem

(c) 35. The _____ is a major relay station for sensory pathways from sensory organs to the forebrain; it is hidden in the center of the brain.

(a) medulla
(b) cerebellum
(c) thalamus
(d) brainstem

(b) 36. The _____ is a finely-fissured structure of two hemispheres; it forms part of the human motor control system and is implicated in neural circuits for classical conditioning.

(a) medulla
(b) cerebellum
(c) thalamus
(d) brainstem

(a) 37. The _____ is a band of neural circuits responsible for the organism's state of arousal.

(a) reticular system
(b) limbic system
(c) hippocampus
(d) hypothalamus

(b) 38. _____ are the elevations on the surface of the cortex.

- (a) fissures
- (b) gyri
- (c) sulci
- (d) a and c above

(c) 39. Turner and Greenough (1985) raised one group of rats in a stimulating environment and another group of rats in a boring environment. The rats raised in the stimulating environment had ____ the second group.

- (a) fewer capillaries and smaller brain surface area than
- (b) more capillaries and a smaller brain surface area than
- (c) more capillaries and a larger brain surface area than
- (d) the same number of capillaries and brain surface area as

(c) 40. In an effort to curtail severe epileptic seizures, the patient H.M. underwent bilateral temporal lobe resection. As a result of this surgery, H.M. lost his ability

- (a) to remember new facts even for a very short period of time
- (b) to remember events from the distant past
- (c) to remember new facts for long periods of time
- (d) to acquire new motor skills such as mirror drawing

(d) 41. There are different forms of long-term potentiation (LTP) in the hippocampus, including associative LTP. Associative LTP involves the joint stimulation of

- (a) two long pathways to a neuron
- (b) two strong pathways to a neuron
- (c) two weak pathways to a neuron
- (d) a weak and a strong pathway to a neuron

(a) 42. The brain structure which has been implicated in the transfer of information from short-term memory to long-term memory is the

- (a) hippocampus
- (b) prefrontal region
- (c) frontal lobe
- (d) halamus

(d) 43. In one study of spatial learning, O'Keefe and Dostoyevsky (1971) noted that rats had specific pyramidal cells that were sensitive to unique locations in space. These cells

- (a) lessened the effects of a lesion to the hippocampus
- (b) limited the rats' ability to complete radial mazes
- (c) xist in rats and other rodents but not in primates
- (d) are termed place cells and are located in the hippocampus

(d) 44. The sensorimotor area, located across from the motor area in the frontal lobe, receives projections from the body surface. Scientists have found that

    (a) larger body parts have more receptors in the motor and sensory control areas than smaller body parts
    (b) larger body parts have less receptors in the motor and sensory controlareas than smaller body parts
    (c) larger body parts have an equal number of receptors in the motor and sensory control areas as smaller body parts
    (d) there is no correlation between the size of a body part and its representation in the motor and sensory control areas

(c) 45. The hippocampus plays an intricate part in diverse learning and memory functions; however, it does not participate in all learning and remembering activities. Which of these statements is **true** about the hippocampus?

    (a) The hippocampus is a principal storage site for declarative memories.
    (b) The hippocampus plays an active role in learning nondeclarative skills.
    (c) The hippocampus is implicated in the consolidation of memories over time.
    (d) The hippocampus is the principal store for implicit memories.

(b) 46. The _____ occupy the posterior top of the cortex. Their function includes somatic sensations and the integration of sensory and visual information.

    (a) temporal lobes
    (b) parietal lobes
    (c) frontal lobes
    (d) occipital lobes

(a) 47. The following lobes contain the primary auditory cortex, process visual information, and are involved in memory and attention operations.

    (a) temporal lobes
    (b) parietal lobes
    (c) frontal lobes
    (d) occipital lobes

(b) 48. The _____ is a transmission site of visual information; it receives input from the retina and passes it along to the visual cortex in the occipital lobe.

    (a) medial geniculate body
    (b) lateral geniculate body
    (c) projection area
    (d) association area

(c) 49. Not all ganglion cells have the same response patterns to light stimuli projecting to their receptive fields. If a ganglion cell is an "off-center, on-surround" cell,

    (a) light in the periphery and light projected to the center would decrease the cell's firing rate
    (b) light in the periphery and central light projected to the center would increase the cell's firing rate
    (c) light in the periphery would increases firing and light projected to the would decreases the cell's firing rate
    (d) light in the periphery would decrease firing and light projected to the center would increases the cell's firing rate

CHAPTER 3

(c) 1. William James was among the first psychologists to address the topic of attention. He concluded that attention

    (a) is based on a filtering system in short-term memory
    (b) is automatic and does not require a conscious effort
    (c) is based on neural processes in the brain
    (d) requires an effort and results in the expansion of one's mental focus to perceive several stimuli simultaneously

(a) 2. The methods of limits is one of the psychophysical methods. It involves the following procedure

    (a) the experimenter presents a sequence of stimuli changing along an intensity continuum. The subject makes a Yes-response when s/he detects the stimulus, otherwise s/he makes a No-response
    (b) the experimenter presents signal and blank trials. The subject makes a Yes-response when she detects a stimulus, otherwise she makes a No-response
    (c) the experimenter presents signal and blank trials and manipulates the payoff-schedule. The subject makes a Yes-response when she detects a stimulus, otherwise she makes a No-response
    (d) none of the above

(c) 3. Psychophysicists found that the probability of Yes-responses

    (a) increases abruptly between stimuli that are detected and those that are not
    (b) depends on the subjects' response criterion
    (c) increases continuously as the stimulus intensity increases
    (d) increases as the payoff for Yes-responses increases

(b) 4. According to the theory of signal detection, the detection of stimuli depends on the following factors

    (a) the experimenter's payoff-schedule and the subject's response bias
    (b) the subject's sensitivity and his/her response bias
    (c) the experimenter's payoff-schedule and the subject's sensitivity
    (d) the probability of signal-plus-noise trials relative to the probability of noise trials

(c) 5. Signal detection experiments include the following types of trials

    (a) detection trials, choice trials
    (b) signal trials, signal-and-noise trials
    (c) noise trials, signal-and-noise trials
    (d) noise trials, detection trials

(c) 6. Signal-detection theory makes the following assumption about the typical distribution of responses

    (a) there is one normal distribution that includes the probability of both Yes- and No-responses
    (b) there are two non-overlapping distributions, one for Yes-responses and the other for No-responses
    (c) there are two overlapping distributions, one for Yes-responses and the other for No-responses
    (d) there are two overlapping distributions, one for Hit-responses and the other for False Alarm responses

(a) 7. The Receiver Operating Characteristic (ROC) is a plot of

    (a) the probability of Hit-responses as a function of False-Alarm probability
    (b) the probability of Hit-responses as a function of stimulus intensity
    (c) the probability of Yes-responses as a function of exposure duration
    (d) the probability of Hit-responses as a function of the payoff-schedule

(d) 8. Signal-detection theory is significant because it

    (a) introduced the difference threshold, in addition to the absolute threshold first proposed by the psychophysicists
    (b) introduced the blank-trials procedure to assess response bias and sensitivity
    (c) introduced payoff schedules to manipulate response bias
    (d) replaced the concept of threshold with a continuous measure of sensitivity

(d) 9. The researcher who advanced the study of early visual processing was

    (a) James
    (b) Cherry
    (c) Broadbent
    (d) Sperling

(b) 10. In the partial reporting procedure the subject

    (a) sees a smaller subset of letters than in the whole reporting procedure
    (b) sees the same size set of letters as in the whole reporting procedure
    (c) sees a different set of symbols than in the whole reporting procedure
    (d) none of the above

(a) 11. According to Neisser, iconic memory refers to the processor that handles early visual information. Iconic memory

    (a) has a relatively large capacity
    (b) has a relatively small capacity
    (c) represents a unique mechanism of attention
    (d) facilitates the process of signal detection

(c) 12. Estimates of the number of items subjects have seen are typically greater in

    (a) the signal-detection procedure than in the method of limits
    (b) the whole reporting procedure than in the partial reporting procedure
    (c) the partial reporting procedure than in the whole reporting procedure
    (d) the partial reporting procedure than in the visual search task

(b) 13. Cherry's dichotic listening experiments yielded the following results

    (a) subjects understood messages presented to both ears provided they were important
    (b) subjects understood messages to the attended ear having little knowledge of information presented to the nonattended ear
    (c) subjects understood messages to the attended ear and remembered some of the information presented to the nonattended ear
    (d) subjects applied different response criteria to the information presented via the attended and nonattended channels

(a) 14. According to Broadbent's influential filtering theory,

    (a) the filtering mechanism intervenes between the detection and recognition stages
    (b) the filtering mechanism precedes both the detection and recognition stages
    (c) the filtering mechanism follows upon both the detection and recognition stages
    (d) filtering accuracy depends on the type of information presented to the listener

(b) 15. According to Broadbent's influential filtering theory, filtering

    (a) is based on semantic attributes of the input
    (b) is based on physical attributes of the input
    (c) is a function of the payoff schedule

(d) is independent of the total information load

(d) 16. The theorist who proposed an early filter in the information processing system was

   (a) Shiffrin
   (b) Cherry
   (c) Sperling
   (d) Broadbent

(d) 17. Results from memory search tasks and visual search tasks are best captured in the following statement

   (a) in both tasks, reaction times increase as a function of the size of the memory set
   (b) in both tasks, reaction times are independent of the size of the memory set
   (c) reaction times increase as a function of the memory set in visual searches, but not in memory searches
   (d) reaction times increase as a function of the memory set in memory searches, but not in visual searches

(b) 18. Schneider and Shiffrin's (1977) multiple-frame task involved two trial types, consistent and inconsistent, and two classes of stimuli, letters and digits.

   (a) on consistent trials, targets and distractors were selected from the same stimulus class
   (b) on consistent trials, targets and distractors were selected from different stimulus classes
   (c) on inconsistent trials, letter and digit frames were alternated
   (d) on inconsistent trials, subjects received inconsistent feedback

(a) 19. The pattern of reaction times (RTs) in Schneider and Shiffrin's (1977) experiment is best summarized by the following statement

   (a) RTs increased as a function of memory set size in the inconsistent condition, but not in the consistent condition
   (b) RTs increased as a function of memory set size in the consistent condition, but not in the inconsistent condition
   (c) RTs were independent of memory set size in both conditions
   (d) the pattern of RTs was a function of serial search processes

(c) 20. According to Treisman's theory of feature integration

   (a) object perception is immediate
   (b) feature detection precedes feature recognition
   (c) feature integration follows upon feature detection
   (d) detection and integration of features are part of the same process

(a) 21. According to Treisman's theory of feature integration the following results would be expected

    (a) a letter moving on a screen is difficult to spot among stationary distractors
    (b) any moving object should be easy to spot among stationary distractors
    (c) the detection time of a moving object is inversely related to the number of distractors
    (d) none of the above

(d) 22. The waterfall illusion illustrates the following perceptual phenomenon

    (a) sensitivity
    (b) response bias
    (c) filtering
    (d) none of the above

(b) 23. According to neuroscientists, neural feature processing is

    (a) dependent
    (b) independent
    (c) rapid
    (d) sensitive to downward motion

(d) 24. Consider a task in which a subject searches for the letter X in an array of distractor letters. According to the Similarity Theory of Visual Search, locating the letter X would be easier to distinguish when the set of

    (a) targets are large
    (b) distractors are small
    (c) targets and distractors are the same
    (d) targets and distractors are different

(a) 25. Consider a task in which a subject searches for the letter X in an array of distractor letters. According to the Similarity Theory of Visual Search, locating the letter X would be more difficult when

    (a) distractors are similar to one another
    (b) distractors are dissimilar
    (c) distractors are large
    (d) distractors are small

(b) 26. McLeod's Movement Filter Theory suggests that organisms have a special mechanism that detects movement independently of other stimuli in the visual field. The movement filter

    (a) triggers neurons in the visual pathway
    (b) warns organisms of approaching animals
    (c) distinguishes fast moving from slow moving objects
    (d) is localized in the parietal lobe

(a) 27. Posner's Spatial Cuing Task provides the subject with visual cues and targets that flash on a computer screen. On some trials the cues predicted the target location correctly; on others they did not. Knowing the target location enhances a person's spatial attention. According to Posner, spatial attention

   (a) leads to a faster reaction on valid, but not on invalid trials
   (b) is based on anticipatory overt eye movements
   (c) is uniformly distributed over the visual field
   (d) is influenced by an appropriate pay-off schedule

(c) 28. Disengagement of attention is the ability to disengage from the location indicated by a prompting cue in the visual field and shift to a new focus. The neural structure that supports the attentional disengagement mechanism is thought to be the _____.

   (a) cerebral hemisphere
   (b) temporal lobe
   (c) parietal region
   (d) occipital region

(d) 29. In the Stroop Task the subject is given a list of color names. The subject must either read the words or name the color of the printed words. The Stroop Task illustrates that

   (a) it is easier to identify colors with shorter words
   (b) it is easier to identify colors with longer words
   (c) two aspects in the stimulus complement each other
   (d) two aspects in the stimulus compete with each other

(b) 30. When subjects who were reading a book were interrupted by oddball stimuli, Näätänen found that

   (a) ERP levels remained the same
   (b) ERP levels increased
   (c) ERP levels decreased
   (d) ERP levels increased for a few seconds and then leveled off

(c) 31. Although research on attention has generated many different paradigms and models, different attention frameworks agree that

   (a) with practice the human mind can control any number of tasks at a time
   (b) attentional control is located in the occipital region
   (c) the human information processing system has a limited capacity
   (d) all of the above

(b) 32. William James said all of the following about the physiological conditions of attention except

    (a) in all probability, there must be an increased bloodflow to the cortex
    (b) there is an inverse relationship between attention and interest
    (c) the appropriate cortical center must be excited before attention can take place
    (d) the sense-organ must adapt itself to the clearest reception of the object

(d) 33. Resource allocation is necessary when

    (a) concentrating on one stimulus rather than another
    (b) trying to find a target among a set of objects
    (c) executing two tasks at once
    (d) all of the above

(a) 34. Fechner is one of the founders of psychophysics. He has also been credited for his research on the

    (a) threshold of sensitivity
    (b) ROC curve
    (c) movement filter
    (d) sensory gain hypothesis

(c) 35. Assume a subject is participating in a signal detection experiment. She is given a dime for each hit. According to the response bias principle, a subject is likely to respond on a blank trial. Her response is called a

    (a) miss
    (b) hit
    (c) false alarm
    (d) correct rejection

(c) 36. If the Receiver Operating Characteristic (ROC) curve is below the diagonal, we may conclude that

    (a) there were more hits than false alarms in the experiment
    (b) there were as many hits as false alarms in the experiment
    (c) there were more false alarms than hits in the experiment
    (d) the subject was paid off for each hit she signaled

(a) 37. Sperling designed the partial reporting procedure. This task consisted of flashing a matrix of letters to the subject and having him report a subset of these letters, according to a cue that followed the presentation of the letter matrix. According to Chapter 3, which of the following is not a cue that Sperling used?

- (a) a number on the computer screen
- (b) a high-pitched tone
- (c) a color
- (d) a low-pitched tone

(d) 38. Sperling's experiment on partial reporting technique suggests that more information is available to the subjects than they can report. This suggested to Neisser (1967) that the information is held in

- (a) echoic memory
- (b) iconic memory
- (c) partial visual processing
- (d) signal detection decay

(d) 39. Using the partial reporting procedure, Sperling presented the reporting cue at several time intervals after stimulus onset. At which of the following intervals was a greater percentage of letters recalled than in the whole reporting condition?

- (a) 100 milliseconds
- (b) 500 milliseconds
- (c) 500 and 1000 milliseconds
- (d) 100 and 500 milliseconds

(d) 40. Cherry (1953) conducted research on dichotic listening. In such research the subject

- (a) is presented with two different stimuli in each ear
- (b) attended to one stimulus and not the other
- (c) detected and recognized both of the stimuli
- (d) all of the above

(b) 41. Broadbent (1958) postulated a component early in the system that analyzes the input in terms of its constituents, such as physical features and the gender and dialect of a voice. He also proposed that the stimulus receives further analysis. "Further analysis" means

- (a) detection of the second, or unattended, stimulus
- (b) fuller recognition of sound features and interpretation of the message
- (c) analysis of the auditory stimuli that the subject perceives
- (d) paying attention to two different tasks at once

(a) 42. According to Neisser (1967), which of the following analyzes simple features of a visual stimulus, such as length, orientation, and color, etc?

- (a) automatic processes
- (b) attentive processes
- (c) dichotic filter
- (d) further analysis

(b) 43. According to Neisser (1967), which of the following registers spatial relations between features and synthesizes an object from a perceived stimulus?

- (a) automatic processes
- (b) attentive processes
- (c) further analysis
- (d) movement filter

(c) 44. Schneider and Shiffrin (1977) conducted research using the memory search and visual search paradigms. They used a multiple-frame search task and varied the size of the memory set and the relation between targets and distractors. Their study consisted of a series of consistent and inconsistent trials. Results of their study suggest that

- (a) subjects complete both the consistent and inconsistent condition via a parallel search
- (b) the consistent condition elicits a serial search while the inconsistent condition elicits a parallel search
- (c) the consistent condition elicits a parallel search while the inconsistent condition elicits a serial search
- (d) both the consistent and the inconsistent conditions trigger a serial search

(c) 45. Treisman (1988) postulated that perceptual experience is based on feature detection and feature integration. She suggested that the primary salient features we detect in an object are all of the following except

- (a) colors
- (b) distance
- (c) lines
- (d) size

(b) 46. Treisman's conjunction hypothesis stated that

- (a) color is not perceived as a salient feature
- (b) it is more difficult to find a white square among a set of black squares and white circles than if among a set of black squares and black circles
- (c) it is more difficult to find a white triangle among a set of black squares and white circles than among a set of white squares and black triangles
- (d) rotated T's are easier to detect than upright T's

(a) 47. Treisman's theory of feature detection and feature integration was criticized because

  (a) some conjoined features are easy to detect
  (b) it takes the same amount of time to identify distractors among a set of targets no matter how different or similar targets and distractors are
  (c) she did not validate her experimental results against a formal model
  (d) conjunctive search is always serial

(b) 48. Posner (1980) adopted a type of signal detection paradigm to demonstrate the advantage of knowing the target locations in the following task

  (a) the feature recognition task
  (b) the spatial cuing task
  (c) the attentive processing task
  (d) the feature integration task

(c) 49. Mangun and Hillyard (1990) proposed the sensory gain hypothesis according to which spatial attention produces all of the following effects, except

  (a) increases attention in the visual pathways
  (b) attracts attention to the stimulus and enhances sensory input
  (c) increases activity in the left hemisphere when the stimulus is seen in the left visual field
  (d) enhances activity in the prestriate cortex

(b) 50. According to Chapter 3, which of the following structures does not play a role in visual attention?

  (a) the posterior parietal lobe
  (b) the inferior olive
  (c) pulvinar nucleus in the thalamus
  (d) the prestriate cortex

(d) 51. Näätänen (1990) experimented with single-task situations and oddball stimuli, and with dual-tasks situations. The findings of his experiment on mismatch negativity led him to conclude that

  (a) subjects' attention is so devoted to the primary task that they do not notice an oddball stimulus
  (b) recordings did not reflect any measurable response to the oddball stimulus
  (c) ERP patterns of subjects in dual-task situations differed from ERP patterns of control subjects
  (d) a secondary task is always detected and analyzed by an automatic process

(c) 52. Attention researchers have examined automatization in the dual-task paradigm. Which of the following is not a consequence of automatization?

    (a) gains are large early in practice and diminish later
    (b) execution of a task requires less effort because the person has more than one way of doing it
    (c) performance diminishes in quality
    (d) performance occurs without the person's intention

(a) 53. Posner et al. (1990) examined patients with lesioned parietal lobes. The researchers discovered that these patients

    (a) were slower than normal subjects on invalid trials, but had almost equal reaction times as normal subjects on valid trials
    (b) performed as well as subjects with "normal" or unlesioned brains
    (c) had difficulty identifying a target in the spatial attention task
    (d) were slower than normal subjects on identifying a target in valid trials, but had almost equal reaction times as normal subjects on invalid trials

(b) 54. Which of the following is an example of the Stroop effect?

    (a) reading a word in the left visual field, while reading another word in the right visual field at the same time
    (b) reading a color name printed in a different color
    (c) identifying small letters as part of a geometric figure
    (d) recalling one's home phone number while in the office

(d) 55. Based on attention research we may conclude all of the following except

    (a) the human information processing system cannot process all of the information arriving through the perceptual organs
    (b) because of processing limits, a person devotes more attention to the attended task than to other aspects of task environment
    (c) attention necessary for a task depends on how well-practiced it is
    (d) attention is facilitated by increased blood flow to the parietal lobe

(c) 56. Increased activity in the extrastriate cortex, measured by a PET scan during a feature integration task, would support which theory:

    (a) Broadbent's
    (b) James'
    (c) Treisman's
    (d) Schneider and Shiffrin's

(b) 57. According to Posner, the orienting network of attention involves three neural structures, which are implicated in overt and covert attention processes, these are: the parietal lobes, the superior colliculus, and

- (a) the ventricle
- (b) the thalamus
- (c) the occipital lobe
- (d) the corpus callosum

(a) 58. In patients with parietal lesions, case studies have found visual neglect and slowed response to invalid trials with cues projected to the damaged parietal lobe. Posner and his colleagues reasoned this area is responsible for the:

- (a) disengagement of attention
- (b) reaction time
- (c) shifting attention
- (d) filtering of information

(d) 59. According to Posner, the executive network of attention exercises a control function in target detection, however a price is paid for focused attention.

- (a) Interference in increased from other signals
- (b) It is harder to concentrate
- (c) Selective attention is more difficult
- (d) Concentration on a mental task may decrease external stimulus tracking

(c) 60. Marcel (1983) flashed the word *butter* very briefly on a screen followed by a mask, so that subjects were unaware of seeing it. Subjects recognized words related to *butter* that were presented subsequently, more rapidly than control words.

- (a) This indicates some people read rapidly
- (b) This means that Pavlovian response occurs in humans
- (c) This suggests we may perceive stimuli without awareness.
- (d) This is an illustration of blindsight

(b) 61. Gopher (1993) used a computer game to simulate a multiple task condition, where obstacles suddenly cropped up on the screen and had to be dealt with. He found that

- (a) students love video games
- (b) students were initially panicked
- (c) training made no difference to scores
- (d) the control group did better in actual training flights

(a) 62. Blindsight is observed in patients with visual center lesions. They can guess "unseen" objects with greater than expected accuracy. This would be an example of:

- (a) perception without consciousness
- (b) mind over matter
- (c) implicit memory
- (d) increased sensitivity

CHAPTER 4

(d) 1. The record of photograph patterns of energy associated with speech sounds is termed a "sound spectrogram." Spectrograms of real speech usually show

- (a) specific sine wave patterns for words
- (b) discrete phonemes
- (c) discernible boundaries between words
- (d) formants overlapping word boundaries.

(c) 2. The word superiority effect illustrates how several sources of information can simultaneously suggest one interpretation of a target while excluding other interpretations. This concept is termed

- (a) bottom-up processing
- (b) top-down processing
- (c) constraint satisfaction
- (d) target agreement

(b) 3. McClelland and Rumelhart (1981) developed a network model to simulate word and letter recognition. Which of these assumptions are **not** made by the network model?

- (a) There are three levels of analysis: words, letters, and features
- (b) Levels of analysis act independently of neighboring levels.
- (c) Units of the stimulus are represented by nodes in the network.
- (d) There are connections between nodes.

(c) 4. The activation of a node is influenced by the input from other nodes via connections. In general, a connection between two units is _____ when the two nodes _____ with each other.

- (a) excitatory; are inconsistent
- (b) inhibitory; are consistent
- (c) excitatory; are consistent
- (d) inhibitory; interact

(a) 5. There were two classes of recognition theories described in chapter 4: interactive and modular approaches. Search theory of word recognition is known as a modular recognition theory because

    (a) letter recognition and word recognition are executed by separate processors
    (b) word recognition is independent of the component letters
    (c) letter recognition includes both bottom-up and top-down information
    (d) the word frequency effect cannot be explained by the search theory

(b) 6. Biederman (1990) proposed four invariant properties of boundaries that define regions. Two or more edges meeting in a common junction, such as the letter "Y", is an example of

    (a) smooth continuation
    (b) cotermination
    (c) parallelism
    (d) symmetry

(c) 7. David Marr introduced difference operators as part of his computer vision system. Difference operators fulfil the following function

    (a) they evaluate the difference between correct recognition responses and false alarms
    (b) they compute the difference in activation between various interpretations of the stimulus
    (c) they compute the difference in brightness between regions
    (d) they operate on different channels of the visual system

(b) 8. The core of Marr's algorithm of computer vision is

    (a) The primal sketch
    (b) a process of converting signals into symbols
    (c) the application of difference operators
    (d) the interpretation of the visual image

(d) 9. According to Neisser's influential theory of recognition, the recognition process is based on

    (a) interpreting an input in terms of its context
    (b) selecting the most plausible interpretation of a stimulus
    (c) identifying the constituent components of a stimulus and matching them to templates
    (d) establishing a link between the encoded stimulus and its mental representation

(d) 10. According to template theory, recognition of a stimulus involves

    (a) identifying the components of a stimulus matching each to a template
    (b) identifying the features of a stimulus and integrating them into a template
    (c) finding the structural description that fits the input stimulus
    (d) none of the above

(d) 11. The Pandemonium model involves the following levels of analysis

    (a) feature, symbolic, cognitive, and template analysis
    (b) sensory, symbolic, cognitive, and decision analysis
    (c) image, descriptive, and cognitive analysis
    (d) sensory, features, cognitive, and decision analysis

(d) 12. The more successful models of the recognition process include structural descriptions. Such descriptions have proved useful because they

    (a) manage to incorporate all details in the input stimulus
    (b) represent an efficient formalization of the template that matches the stimulus
    (c) are abstract and symbolic accounts of the relation between input and representation
    (d) reflect the relations between the components of the input

(c) 13. Posner and Mitchell (1967) found in their letter matching task that subjects required 70 ms less to judge a pair of identical letters like *AA* than a pair like *Aa*. They attributed the additional processing time for the latter pair to the time

    (a) it took subjects to develop a structural description of the letters
    (b) required to transform the capital letter into the small letter
    (c) to retrieve the names of the letters
    (d) none of the above

(d) 14. A phoneme is defined as the

    (a) the basic unit of speech sounds
    (b) the feature that is invariant among similar speech sounds
    (c) a measure of the intensity and frequency of speech sounds
    (d) the smallest unit of sound that differentiates among words

(a) 15. Speech sounds are produced by different components of the speech tract, different levels of air pressure, and resonance. Speech sounds differ on the following dimensions

    (a) manner of articulation, place of articulation, voicing
    (b) manner of articulation, number of formants, direction of formant transition
    (c) voicing, number of formants, relative location of formants
    (d) place of articulation, number of formants, relative location of formants

(b) 16. According to the motor theory of speech perception

    (a) each species of primates has a developed a characteristic system of speech sounds
    (b) speech sounds are recognized because listeners implicitly re-enact the production of the sound
    (c) the production and comprehension of speech sounds are based on different processing structures
    (d) the perception of a speech sound is related to its context

(c) 17. According to research on letter recognition, recognition of the letter B

    (a) is best when it is presented individually, for example, B
    (b) is best when it forms part of a pronounceable letter string, for example, MALB
    (c) is best when it forms part of a word as in LAMB
    (d) is independent of the mode of presentation

(a) 18. McClelland and Rumelhart's model of letter and word recognition

    (a) accounts for the word superiority effect by assuming that target letters receive both bottom-up and top-down activation
    (b) accounts for the word superiority effect by considering the word context in interpreting individual letters
    (c) accounts for the word superiority effect by including the feature and letter levels of analysis and by assuming that they interact
    (d) does not address the word superiority effect because it was developed for realistic recognition situations which always involve a full context

(d) 19. The following statement characterizes spoken word recognition

    (a) because echoic memory lasts relatively long, spoken word identification typically takes up to a second
    (b) is initiated after the listener has heard all of the phonemes of the word
    (c) unlike recognition of printed words, spoken word recognition is facilitated by the linguistic context
    (d) is an on-line process

(a) 20. Recognition-by-Components theory (RBC) states that

    (a) an object is recognized by identifying its geons
    (b) an object is identified by tracing its outline
    (c) a shape is recognized by matching its features to prototypical components
    (d) a shape is recognized by detecting its edges and by forming regions

(c) 21. According to the Recognition-by-Components theory object recognition occurs when

    (a) all components of an object have been identified
    (b) the boundaries of the object match the object's prototype in memory
    (c) the critical geons have been identified
    (d) the relation of edges and joints has been interpreted

(a) 22. According to the Recognition-by-Components theory,

    (a) complex objects are recognized more quickly than simple objects
    (b) simple objects are recognized more quickly than complex objects
    (c) two-dimensional shapes are recognized more quickly than three-dimensional objects

(d) three-dimensional objects are recognized more quickly than two-dimensional shapes

(b) 23. According to Biederman, our recognition of degraded objects

(a) requires long-term memory
(b) is easier when joints are included on the diagram
(c) is easier when attention is drawn to the shading of the objects
(d) becomes more efficient with age

(d) 24. Rhodes' study of facial recognition compared recognition of caricatures and veridical drawings. Rhodes found

(a) that subjects' recognition accuracy for caricatures is less
(b) that subjects' recognition accuracy for drawings is less
(c) that subjects recognize drawings faster
(d) that subjects recognize caricatures faster

(c) 25. The first stage of David Marr's model of computer vision involves several steps. Which of the following represents the order of those steps?

(a) the image is acquired, the line sketch is developed, the image is cleaned up, the edges are detected
(b) the image is acquired, the edges are detected, the image is cleaned up, the edges are detected
(c) the image is acquired, the image is cleaned up, the edges are detected, a line sketch is developed
(d) the image is acquired, the edges are detected, the line sketch is developed, the image is cleaned up

(c) 26. What is the function of difference operators in David Marr's model of pattern recognition?

(a) they assess the difference between the description of a stimulus and its stored representation
(b) look for different templates that match the captured stimulus
(c) compute the difference in brightness between stimulus regions
(d) take the primal sketch of a stimulus and match it to an encoded memory

(c) 27. A difficulty for the template theory of human pattern recognition is that

(a) it does not take letters into account
(b) it is not clear how templates are stored in long term memory
(c) it is inflexible in terms of recognizing unique stimuli
(d) it does not specify where the representations are stored

(b) 28. The designers of the Pandemonium model invented characters or demons to analyze four levels of feature detection. Which of the following is the correct order in which the demons operate?

  (a) feature demons, image demons, cognitive demons, decision demon
  (b) image demons, feature demons, cognitive demons, decision demon
  (c) feature demons, cognitive demons, decision demon, image demons
  (d) cognitive demons, feature demons, image demons, decision demon

(c) 29. According to Chapter 4, speech sounds differ in terms of three dimensions. Which of the following is not one of these?

  (a) voicing
  (b) manner of articulation
  (c) pronunciation
  (d) place of articulation

(b) 30. A sound spectrogram is a photographic record of speech sounds. The dark regions on a spectrogram are called formants. A formant

  (a) shows the boundaries between words
  (b) represents energy levels at a certain frequency
  (c) is used to predict categorical perception of speech patterns
  (d) helps researchers find the relation between patterns of acoustic energy and different speech sounds

(d) 31. Liberman and his colleagues proposed the motor theory of speech perception. According to this theory, speech sounds are recognized by

  (a) matching them with prototypes in long term memory
  (b) initial feature analysis in different parts of the brain and subsequent synthesis
  (c) analyzing their constituent formants
  (d) implicitly producing the sound

(a) 32. Van Lancker and her colleagues conducted a study on brain-damaged patients. Their results suggest that lesions in the left hemisphere of the brain

  (a) produce language disorders such as aphasia
  (b) make voice recognition difficult
  (c) make rhythmic patterns of sound indistinguishable from one another
  (d) prevent the recognition of musical sounds

(c) 33. According to the word superiority effect, letters are best recognized if they are presented

  (a) alone
  (b) through a tachistoscope
  (c) embedded in a word
  (d) among a string of letters

(b) 34. McClelland and Rumelhart's (1981) model of word recognition assumes that

    (a) there are four levels of analyses that all interact
    (b) units of stimulus are represented by nodes in the network
    (c) an embedded word is recognized because of constraint satisfaction
    (d) all levels of analysis receive some degree of activation

(d) 35. In recognizing spoken words, the cohort model suggests that

    (a) several sources of information communicate in order to respond to the stimulus
    (b) words are best understood when the entire sentence is in order
    (c) the more practice one dedicates to listening to words, the more automatic word recognition becomes
    (d) a word is recognized by elimination of other candidates

(c) 36. Biederman (1990) suggests that humans recognize shapes by means of identifying their components. He called these components

    (a) configurations
    (b) blocks
    (c) geons
    (d) features

(c) 37. Which of the following is not a Gestalt principle?

    (a) proximity
    (b) closure
    (c) superiority
    (d) continuation

(b) 38. Suppose a circle is drawn on the blackboard, and there is a gap in the perimeter. Nevertheless this entity is a circle. This illustrates the Gestalt principle of

    (a) continuation
    (b) closure
    (c) similarity
    (d) proximity

(c) 39. According to Biederman's Recognition-by-Components theory, the geon alphabet includes the following number of geons.

    (a) 15
    (b) 16
    (c) 24
    (d) 36

(c) 40. According to the recognition by components theory, geons identify the following property (properties)

   (a) shading
   (b) texture
   (c) shape
   (d) all of the above

(b) 41. According to Biederman's recognition by components theory, object complexity and object recognition are related as follows

   (a) the more geons are in an object, the more difficult the object is to recognize
   (b) complex objects are recognized more quickly than simple objects
   (c) a complex object requires more steps in the recognition process than a simple object
   (d) a complex object is recognized by the tracing of its contours, whereas a simple object is recognized by its basic constituents

(d) 42. Johansson had observers look at lights attached to people who executed certain movements in the dark. His research

   (a) supports Biederman's recognition by components approach
   (b) indicates that we recognize faces better if the person is smiling
   (c) suggests that recognition of complex movements is faster than that of simple ones
   (d) demonstrates event perception

(c) 43. The term "prosopagnosia" refers to the inability to recognize

   (a) phonemes
   (b) words
   (c) faces
   (d) visual stimuli in general

(d) 44. There are a few types of muscles which make up the almost 800 muscles within the human body. The _____ muscles, for example, control the movement of the body's internal organs.

   (a) motor
   (b) skeletal
   (c) striped
   (d) smooth

(c) 45. Muscles are an essential component of the movement system, representing the effector organs of the motor system. Which of the following statements is **not** true about muscles?

   (a) Muscles can only contract.
   (b) Muscle contraction produces kinetic energy.
   (c) Muscles with fewer axons produce finer movement.
   (d) Muscles are innervated to varying degrees by the axons of motor neurons.

(d) 46. The word cerebellum means "small brain" in Latin; however, its role in movement is far from small. Which of these functions is **not** performed by the cerebellum?

- (a) coordination of motor movements
- (b) control of the muscle tone
- (c) contribution to motor learning
- (d) planning the time sequence of movements

(a) 47. Parkinson's disease is a condition afflicting mostly elderly patients. Motor control in Parkinson's patients is dysfunctional due to impairments to the

- (a) basal ganglia
- (b) cerebellum
- (c) prefrontal cortex
- (d) premotor cortex

(c) 48. Two physicians, Fritsch and Hitzig, applied electrical stimulation to the motor cortex in dogs. Based on their experiments they hypothesized that damage to the right motor hemisphere would

- (a) cause a human patient to confuse the order of the constituent components of a motor act
- (b) cause the patient to experience tremors of the hands at rest
- (c) affect movement in the limbs of the patient's left side
- (d) paralyze the patient's right side

(c) 49. The premotor cortex is believed to help govern the temporal sequence of motor acts. In the premotor area, neurons

- (a) control individual muscles
- (b) control individual muscle groups
- (c) govern global movement towards a target
- (d) are activated after movements relative to a specific location are begun

(a) 50. Georgopoulos and his research team found that in monkeys, different cell groups in motor cotex were maximally responsive for movements in a specific direction while participating in lesser degrees in controlling the movement in neighboring directions. This activation pattern of reaching neurons led researchers to formulate the concept of

- (a) population coding
- (b) primary motor cortex
- (c) Fitts' law
- (d) reaching theory

(b) 51. There is a set of disorders which have been attributed to lesions in cortical centers that control motor activation. The disorder is marked by the inability to execute an intended action even when the motor system is intact otherwise. This disorder is known as

- (a) cerebral palsy
- (b) apraxia
- (c) myrasthenia gravis
- (d) multiple sclerosis

(b) 52. Following the lead of Woodworth, the psychologist Paul Fitts formulated Fitts' law. According to this law

- (a) objects are recognized by identifying their constituent geons and the relations among them
- (b) the time to execute a movement increases as a logarithmic function of the difficulty of the movement
- (c) damage in the right hemisphere affects movements in the limbs of the patient's left side
- (d) direct electrical stimulation of specific regions of the motor cortex produces movements in specific body parts

(b) 53. Lashley (1951) noted that in response chaining the time to wait for feedback is simply too long to account for the fast occurrence of movements. For example, when typing the word *epic* the *i* is launched well before the letters *e* and *p* are typed. This is an example of

- (a) serial learning
- (b) coarticulation
- (c) chaining
- (d) response summation

(b) 54. Anderson (1980) viewed the acquisition of motor skills, along with other cognitive skills, in terms of three successive stages. Which of these is **not** one of Anderson's stages?

- (a) cognitive stage
- (b) associative stage
- (c) procedural stage
- (d) autonomous stage

(d) 55. As a result of observing typing speed up to 147 wpm, Lashley (1951) argued that skilled typing necessitate motor control

- (a) with high degrees of freedom
- (b) supported by response chains
- (c) by the prefrontal lobe
- (d) by an abstract schema

(b) 56. Typing is not only very fast but there is a a characteristic pattern of typing speed as a function of the combination of hands and fingers in typing. Which of these statements about typing is **incorrect**?

    (a) Intervals between cross-hand keystrokes are shorter than those for the same hand.
    (b) Lexical information about a word is irrelevant to the planning of a key-press sequence.
    (c) Keystrokes within one hand are a function of the number of fingers involved and the distance between keys.
    (d) About 80% of all typing errors in skilled typists are transposition errors and most of these are cross-hand transpositions.

(a) 57. Rumelhart and Norman (1982) developed a computer simulation where a recognition schema or node exists for each word. The links between word nodes and keypress nodes and the response system are _____; connections between keypress nodes are _____.

    (a) excitatory; inhibitory
    (b) inhibitory; excitatory
    (c) excitatory; also excitatory
    (d) inhibitory; also inhibitory

(c) 58. Researchers have discovered that cortical areas implicated in motor control include the following.

    (a) the parietal, prefrontal, and occipital lobes
    (b) the premotor cortex and the primary motor cortex
    (c) the prefrontal cortex, premotor cortex, and primary motor cortex
    (d) the temporal, premotor cortex, and primary motor cortex

(b) 59. Motor control centers in the cortex and the muscles which are the effectors of movement communicate via

    (a) direct links between cortex and muscles
    (b) the spinal cord and axons coming from the spinal cord
    (c) axons coming from the cerebellum
    (d) all of the above

(a) 60. A team of researchers led by neuroscientist Georgopoulos discovered reaching neurons in the monkey motor cortex. They formulated the concept of population coding to describe the behavior of these neurons. Population coding is an instance of
    (a) a distributed representation
    (b) a symbolic representation
    (c) a localized representation
    (d) parallel processing of a population of neurons

(d) 61. The University of Michigan psychologist Paul Fitts undertook a systematic study of movements aimed at a target. He examined movements as a function of the following variables:

    (a) distance, force
    (b) precision, force
    (c) speed, force
    (d) distance, precision

(b) 62. In their study of motor movements, scientists have sought to find an account of the degrees-of-freedom problem. In this context, "degrees of freedom" refer to

    (a) the number of different movements a given limb can execute
    (b) the number of different ways a movement can be executed
    (c) the number of different muscles that must be coordinated to execute a movement
    (d) the statistical constraints on executing different movements simultaneously

(b) 63. According to Turvey's ecological perspective, the components of the motor system

    (a) are guided by a central executive
    (b) collaborate without an executive
    (c) seek to achieve maximum force in reaching a target
    (d) are subject to external control from the primary motor centers

(d) 64. Rosenbaum's appraoch to the degrees-of-freedom problem is based on the following framework

    (a) the neural network approach
    (b) the connectionist approach
    (c) the ecological approach
    (d) none of the above

CHAPTER 5

(d) 1. Cognitive psychologists distinguish between declarative and procedural knowledge. Declarative knowledge refers to

    (a) our knowledge of facts
    (b) explicit knowledge
    (c) information that is easily expressed
    (d) all of the above

(b) 2. Cognitive psychologists distinguish between declarative and procedural knowledge. Procedural knowledge refers to:

    (a) our knowledge of facts
    (b) implicit knowledge underlying our actions
    (c) knowledge involved in arithmetic operations
    (d) the knowledge used to generate mental images

(a) 3. As its name implies, procedural knowledge involves procedures. Procedures are

    (a) typically represented in terms of production rules
    (b) expressed by defining familiar concepts, describing typical events, and calling up images
    (c) specifically used in executing addition tasks but not in more complex arithmetic operations
    (d) all of the above

(c) 4. Our current understanding of mental representations has been shaped by developments in a variety of disciplines, including philosophy, linguistics, psychology, and computer science. Philosophers distinguish between the following representations

    (a) implicit vs. explicit memory
    (b) analog vs. digital representation
    (c) tacit vs. explicit knowledge
    (d) symbolic vs. propositional logic

(d) 5. A stop sign signifies the command to stop a vehicle. The stop sign represents

    (a) a production
    (b) a proposition
    (c) a predicate
    (d) none of the above

(c) 6. The following is not an instance of procedural knowledge

    (a) comprehending the sentence "Mary is reading a book"
    (b) a math major solving an arithmetic problem
    (c) giving the definition for "table"
    (d) recognizing the letter M

(c) 7. The following term stands for entities other than themselves.

    (a) procedures
    (b) actions
    (c) symbols
    (d) schemas

(a) 8.   The following are considered the fundamental units of thought.

  (a) concepts
  (b) mental models
  (c) propositions
  (d) scripts

(d) 9.   Concepts reduce the multitude of objects, events, and relations in our physical and mental world to a smaller number. The following is true about concepts

  (a) they are defined in terms of themselves
  (b) they stand for something other than themselves
  (c) they are defined in terms of schemas
  (d) they are defined in terms of other concepts

(b) 10.   The following set of models constitutes a major approach to the representation of concepts

  (a) production models
  (b) prototype models
  (c) mental models
  (d) propositional models

(d) 11.   Indicate the attribute that is NOT a part of semantic networks

  (a) classes of objects
  (b) subset membership
  (c) hierarchical relations
  (d) actions

(b) 12.   Semantic networks constitute a major formalism to represent the meaning of concepts. Semantic networks

  (a) describe the conditions and actions implicit in a concept
  (b) allow efficient retrieval of information
  (c) include an information network about a set of visual images
  (d) account for the major empirical effects in the sentence verification paradigm

(d) 13.   Collins and Quillian's semantic network model

  (a) includes a processing model but no structural assumptions
  (b) includes structural assumptions but no processing assumptions
  (c) applies to computers but not humans
  (d) includes processing as well as structural assumptions

(a) 14. Collins and Quillian's network model predicts that

(a) the statement "A dog is a mammal" is verified faster than the statement "A dog is an animal"
(b) the statement "A dog is an animal" is verified faster than the statement "A dog is a mammal"
(c) the statement "A dog is an animal" is verified faster than "A robin is a robin"
(d) the statement "A dog is a robin" is falsified faster than the statement "A dog is an animal" is verified.

(b) 15. According to the semantic network model, sentence verification takes longer the more distant two nodes are in a semantic network. This is called the

(a) fact retrieval effect
(b) category size effect
(c) typicality effect
(d) none of the above

(b) 16. Collins and Quillian's model of semantic memory

(a) accounts successfully for the typicality effect
(b) was based on taxonomic relations
(c) failed to compensate for the distance effect
(d) predicts response times of true and false sentences

(b) 17. Prototype models

(a) represent the meaning of a concept through its association with neighboring concepts and properties
(b) represent the meaning of a concept by defining it in terms of its similarity to an ideal
(c) involve hierarchical relations between concepts
(d) are essentially a variant of the semantic network models

(c) 18. According to Malt and Smith, the similarity between concepts is expressed empirically

(a) by the number of common features of the concepts
(b) by the number of common features plus the number of unique features
(c) by the number of common features less the number of unique features
(d) by the number of instances the concepts share

(a) 19. The following statement characterizes the prototype approach of concept representation. This approach

(a) allows for flexible and imprecise definitions
(b) is advantageous because it captures taxonomic relations
(c) allows the combined representation of declarative and procedural information
(d) is not useful for the representation of concepts denoting social relations

(a) 20. Facts are retrieved in semantic networks

- (a) through spreading activation
- (b) through similarity checking
- (c) by linking features of a concept
- (d) by verifying the most typical properties of the concept

(b) 21. _____ are represented by verbs that link _____ in specific structures.

- (a) events, concepts
- (b) actions; concepts
- (c) concepts, actions
- (d) actions, events

(a) 22. _____ represents a simple idea.

- (a) a proposition
- (b) a concept
- (c) a symbol
- (d) a mental model

(d) 23. A proposition

- (a) is an ordered list of concepts
- (b) may be expressed in terms of networks or as lists
- (c) is either true or false
- (d) all of the above

(a) 24. The expression ____ refers to a general concept and ____ refers to an instance.

- (a) type; token
- (b) token; type
- (c) concept; feature
- (d) feature; concept

(c) 25. A mental representation

- (a) includes the outline of a stimulus
- (b) includes every aspect of a stimulus
- (c) includes a subset of the relations and objects
- (d) indicates the conceptual dependencies supporting an event

(a) 26. Theoretical representations

- (a) are often sparse
- (b) can't predict task performance
- (c) are consciously used by subjects involved in tasks
- (d) represent a person's experience

(a) 27. Cognitive psychologists have proposed several structures to represent our knowledge of events. The following is not used to represent events.

- (a) category
- (b) causal chains
- (c) proposition
- (d) script

(c) 28. Schank's _____ captures the underlying causal links between events.

- (a) sequence of events theory
- (b) causal link theory
- (c) conceptual dependency theory
- (d) semantic network model

(a) 29. Schank's theory shows that each event

- (a) is actually a sequence of events
- (b) occurs independently of each other event
- (c) involves scripts and networks
- (d) is based on condition-action pairs

(b) 30. A stereotypical cluster of events is called

- (a) concept
- (b) script
- (c) schema
- (d) frame

(d) 31. A script

- (a) describes typical events
- (b) has discrete scenes, props, and slots
- (c) allow us to infer actions not explicitly stated in utterances
- (d) all of the above

(a) 32. A _____ is a kind of _____.

- (a) script; schema
- (b) schema; script
- (c) hierarchy; network
- (d) frame; script

(d) 33. Scripts:

- (a) are schemas describing events
- (b) are schemas describing complex objects
- (c) include general information about an event or object
- (d) a & c above

(b) 34. Frames:

- (a) are schemas describing events
- (b) are schemas describing complex objects
- (c) are scripts describing events
- (d) are scripts describing complex objects

(d) 35. Psychologists of the late 19th century believed the following about visual imagery

- (a) it was too subjective a phenomenon to lend itself to scientific scrutiny
- (b) it formed the basis of our abstract thought processes
- (c) researchers measured the notation of visual images in chronometric studies
- (d) researchers debated whether or not thought was imageless

(c) 36. According to such theorists as Paivio, Kosslyn, and Shepard, visual images are _____ representations.

- (a) abstract
- (b) symbolic
- (c) analog
- (d) semantic

(b) 37. Propositions are _____ representations.

- (a) natural
- (b) symbolic
- (c) analog
- (d) veridical

(c) 38. When a mental representation maintains some of the same physical features of the original it is said to be

- (a) abstract
- (b) symbolic
- (c) analog
- (d) natural

(d) 39. A computer includes

   (a) a central processor, memory, and mass storage
   (b) input and output devices
   (c) a video-terminal with a buffer that hold information for a screen image
   (d) all of the above

(d) 40. Kosslyn's CRT theory of visual imagery:

   (a) says that images have a limited capacity
   (b) says that there are two levels of imagery
   (c) combines the analog and the symbolic views of imagery
   (d) all of the above

(b) 41. The _____ of Kosslyn's theory of visual imagery corresponds to the image that we experience, the surface image.

   (a) long-term level
   (b) buffer level
   (c) input level
   (d) none of the above

(d) 42. Which of the following is not an example of declarative knowledge?

   (a) A bird is an animal that flies.
   (b) George Washington was the first president of the United States.
   (c) One plus two equals three.
   (d) The ability to ride a bike.

(a) 43. We often organize the multitude of objects, events, and relations in our physical and mental world into concepts. This ability:

   (a) allows us to know things about objects that are not perceptually apparent
   (b) makes it difficult for us to distinguish between different kinds of similar objects
   (c) forces us to refer to all instances of a category individually, for example, we must differentiate between a tennis ball, a golf ball, and a basket ball
   (d) is lacking in people with certain memory disorders.

(c) 44. When you present a semantic network with the statement "A bloodhound is a dog," activation spreads through the system like water through an irrigation ditch. According to Collins and Quillian, activation spreads from node to node as follows:

   (a) DOG to BLOODHOUND to ANIMAL
   (b) ANIMAL to BLOODHOUND to DOG
   (c) BLOODHOUND to DOG to ANIMAL
   (d) BLOODHOUND to ANIMAL to DOG

(a) 45. Sentence verification times increase with the number of links that intervene between two concepts in a test statement. This is referred to as the

(a) category size effect because larger categories involve more concepts
(b) typicality effect because nodes representing similar objects are found closer together
(c) taxonomic effect because representations are arranged like taxonomies set up by zoologists
(d) prototype effect because concepts are defined in terms of their similarities to an ideal

(c) 46. In order to compensate for the limitations of Collins and Quillian's semantic network model, Malt and Smith (1984) tested subjects using a prototype model. This model:

(a) represented the meaning of concepts through associations with neighboring concepts and properties.
(b) represented the meaning of a concept by defining it in terms of its similarity to an ideal and its place in a hierarchical schema
(c) represented the meaning of concepts by defining them in terms of their similarity to an ideal but not in terms of hierarchical relations
(d) does not explain the typicality effect

(d) 47. Malt and Smith (1984) investigated the relation among concepts via a similarity metric. They found that

(a) sentence verification latencies were independent of the similarity measure
(b) categorization accuracy increased with greater similarity between concepts
(c) categorization latencies increased as a function of the number of unique features
(d) latencies in verification and categorization studies are correlated with the similarity measure

(d) 48. According to Schank (1973), which of the following is not true of a script?

(a) a script has a title and has discrete scenes, props, and slots
(b) a script is a kind of schema that allows us to infer actions not explicitly stated in utterances
(c) a script includes general information about an event or object
(d) a script is a schema describing complex objects

(b) 49. Psychologists of the late 19th century studied ideas, thoughts, and images. They were divided on the question of images: one camp maintained that ideas are accompanied by images, whereas the opposing camp held that thought could be imageless or abstract. It was this controversy about images that contributed to the demise of the introspectionist school and the emergence of behaviorism. The prominent behaviorist at that time was

(a) Roger Shepard
(b) John Watson
(c) Herman Ebbinghaus
(d) Roger Schank

(a) 50. Like other cognitive scientists, Kosslyn (1983) used a computer metaphor of the mind. His theory, the CRT Theory of visual imagery, includes two levels of imagery; the buffer level refers to _____ whereas the long-term level refers to _____.

    (a) the image that we experience; a list that acts like a blueprint for the generation of the image
    (b) the surface image; the image that we experience
    (c) a list of coordinates to indicate the spatial extension of the object; an analog to the imaged object
    (d) the symbolic view of imagery; the analog view of imagery

(c) 51. In her work, Farah (1988) measured Event Related Potentials (ERPs) which differ from the EEG in that:

    (a) they measure all electrical activity in the brain
    (b) they measure blood flow in the visual cortex during visual image tasks
    (c) they measure the electrical activity corresponding to the processing of a specific stimulus
    (d) they are more accurate

(b) 52. According to Johnson-Laird (1983), mental models _____; they encompass more information than events and images in that they include those representations as well as _____.

    (a) transform individual objects into symbolic representations; schemata
    (b) are structural analogues of the environment; the relations between them.
    (c) are a representation of a dynamic environment; schemata
    (d) encompass only a small range of individual representations; the relations between them

(b) 53. Which of the following is untrue about procedural knowledge

    (a) It is surprisingly difficult to express but easy to use.
    (b) Because of its complex makeup, it is more difficult to access.
    (c) Amnesia patients are quite capable of learning new procedural knowledge.
    (d) It is represented in terms of rules.

(d) 54. Production rules:

    (a) are simplifications of an item in short-term memory
    (b) are stored in long-term memory
    (c) contain if-then clauses
    (d) b and c

(c) 55. Neuropsychological case studies have raised the possibility that there may be different memory systems for different concepts, such as animate versus inanimate concepts. This interpretation is problematic, however, because

- (a) brain injury causes general rather than specific memory loss
- (b) case studies are too numerous to be evaluated for a memory model
- (c) there is a possibility of a new memory system with each specific impairment discovered
- (d) memory does not hold concepts in isolation

(d) 56. Kosslyn and colleagues (1993) used PET scan activity to investigate visual perception and visual imaging. They found increased metabolic activity in the parietal and temporal lobes

- (a) only during visual imaging
- (b) only in the control condition
- (c) only during visual perception
- (d) during visual perception and visual imaging

(a) 57. Research has shown changes in anatomical structures and physiological processes, such as increased blood flow activity after_____. This result is consistent with the improved performance found in experts.

- (a) practice
- (b) a rest period
- (c) sleep
- (d) reflection

(b) 58. Adding new and more specific conditions to an existing production rule, allows a learner greater ability to

- (a) generalize
- (b) discriminate
- (c) organize
- (d) sublimate

(c) 59. Researchers represent events in terms of propositions; they represent sequences of events in terms of causal relations. These relations are thought to capture the links between events and the sentence describing the events. Research has shown that sentences are more difficult to remember when subsequent sentences are

- (a) part of a causal chain
- (b) linked to subsequent events
- (c) isolated dead ends
- (d) dependent on prior events

(d) 60. Interestingly, Kerr (1983) found that in mental imagery, people born blind, responded faster to images of large objects than to small ones. Compared to sighted people this is

    (a) inconsistent
    (b) difficult to asses without knowing what they see
    (c) an advance in understanding blindness
    (d) very similar a response

(a) 61. According to Collins and Quillian's network model, in a true or false test, verification of a sentence such as *Coca-cola is blue*, would be

    (a) faster than *Ants are omnivorous*
    (b) difficult to assimilate
    (c) impossible
    (d) an incomplete predicate node

CHAPTER 6

(a) 1. Connectionist networks consist of a large number of small processing units that operate

    (a) in parallel
    (b) independently
    (c) intermittently
    (d) successively

(b) 2. Connectionist networks are a(n)

    (a) adaptation of semantic networks
    (b) adaptation of neural networks
    (c) type of pattern recognition system
    (d) all of the above

(c) 3. Energy passing through connectionist networks is modulated through

    (a) input units
    (b) output units
    (c) connection weights
    (d) all of the above

(b) 4. According to neuroscience research, information in the human brain is stored

    (a) in discrete locations
    (b) across sets of neurons
    (c) in localized areas of the brain
    (d) randomly

(c) 5. According to the Delta procedure, a connectionist network is trained by adjusting the

    (a) input activation to the stimulus strength
    (b) connection weight to the frequency of association
    (c) actual output to the target output
    (d) a & c above

(b) 6. In connectionist networks, memories

    (a) are distributed across different discrete sites
    (b) are overlapping
    (c) are stored at a unique node with a unique set of properties
    (d) none of the above

(d) 7. The term for interpreting and acting on several items of information simultaneously is

    (a) parallel processing
    (b) interactive processing
    (c) Hebbian learning
    (d) constraint satisfaction

(c) 8. How many connections exist in a pattern associator including four input units and four output units? Assume the connectivity scheme introduced in Chapter 6.

    (a) 4
    (b) 8
    (c) 16
    (d) 32

(c) 9. Assume a three-unit network with input units x and y, and output unit z. Assume that the connection weight between unit x and the output unit is 0.1. Further assume a connection weight of 0.2 between units y and z. The input activation level for both input units is 1. If only unit y is activated, the network will produce an output of

    (a) 0.1
    (b) 0.3
    (c) 0.2
    (d) 1.0

(b) 10. Please calculate the input activations of units y and z using the data in the following matrix

	Input		
	y	z	Output
	0.1	0.3	-0.4
	0.5	0.1	-0.6

(a) y = -0.4, z = -0.6
(b) y = -1.0, z = -1.0
(c) y = 1.0, z = 1.0
(d) none of the above

(c) 11. Please calculate the values missing in the following matrix

Input "Popcorn Appearance"

-1	+1	-1	+1	Output "Popcorn Aroma"
-.25	-.25	+.75	-.25	w
-.25	+.75	-.25	-.25	x
-.25	-.25	-.25	+.75	y
+.75	-.25	-.25	-.25	z

(a) w = -1, x = -1, y = +1, z = +1
(b) w = +1, x = +1, y = -1, z = -1
(c) w = -1, x = +1, y = +1, z = -1
(d) w = +1, x = -1, y = -1, z = +1

(a) 12. Complete the following matrix

Input "Chocolate Appearance"

+1   -1   -1   +1
                    Output "Chocolate Aroma"

-.25   +.25   +.25   -.25   -1

-.25   +.25   +.25   -.25   -1

+.25   x   y   +.25   +1

+.25   -.25   -.25   +.25   z

(a) x = -.25; y = -.25; z = +1
(b) x = +.25; y = +.25; z = -1
(c) x = -.25; y = +.25; z = +1
(d) x = -.25; y = -.25; z = -1

(c) 13. The aroma of chocolate is represented in the following matrix by the pattern

Input "Chocolate Appearance"

+1   -1   -1   +1
                    Output "Chocolate Aroma"

-.25   +.25   +.25   -.25   -1

-.25   +.25   +.25   -.25   -1

+.25   x   y   +.25   +1

+.25   -.25   -.25   +.25   z

(a) +1, -1, -1, +1
(b) +.25, -.25, -.25, +.25
(c) -1, -1, +1, z
(d) none of the above

(a) 14. The cells in this matrix represent

Input "Chocolate Appearance"

+1   -1   -1   +1

                                  Output "Chocolate Aroma"

-.25   +.25   +.25   -.25   -1

-.25   +.25   +.25   -.25   -1

+.25   x   y   +.25   +1

+.25   -.25   -.25   +.25   z

- (a) connection strengths
- (b) transfer activations
- (c) connection types
- (d) output activations

(b) 15. Memory retrieval assumes that the association between ____ and ____ was previously established.

- (a) inputs and connection strengths
- (b) inputs and outputs
- (c) connection strengths and outputs
- (d) all of the above

(d) 16. When networks have the capacity to _____ patterns, one network accommodates several input-output associations.

- (a) store
- (b) associate
- (c) reproduce
- (d) superimpose

(b) 17. According to Hebb, the association between two neurons is strengthened when

- (a) both have excitatory connections
- (b) both are active at the same time
- (c) the synaptic connection weight is positive
- (d) all of the above

(a) 18. A value such as the learning rate is known as _____.

   (a) a parameter
   (b) an input strength
   (c) a delta weight
   (d) a coefficient

(b) 19. A parameter is a value that _____ over some test conditions or for some set of subjects.

   (a) increases
   (b) remains constant
   (c) is manipulated
   (d) varies

(d) 20. One reason why Hebbian learning does not work with correlated input patterns is that

   (a) the system is given feedback, but it does not register feedback
   (b) there is no direct relationship between the actual output and the intended target out
   (c) the system adjusts its response to the expected target
   (d) a & b above

(a) 21. In Delta learning, the gap between actual and target output _____ with each additional learning cycle.

   (a) gets smaller
   (b) gets larger
   (c) remains constant
   (d) is manipulated

(c) 22. There are two types of connections in connectionist networks. They are

   (a) inputs and outputs
   (b) address and content
   (c) inhibitory and excitatory
   (d) none of the above

(b) 23. Given the same patterns of input activations, if one were to alter the connection weights, the output _____.

   (a) would remain the same
   (b) would change
   (c) would be reproduced
   (d) a & c above

(a) 24. A _____ has overlapping or superimposed memories. This suggests that memory is represented across a number of storage elements.

   (a) distributed storage system
   (b) serial storage system
   (c) specific storage system
   (d) localized storage system

(d) 25. A connectionist network consists of a large number of small units, which have and do all of the following except

   (a) have an activation level
   (b) collect signals or evidence from all of their neighbors
   (c) produce output based on the signals received
   (d) have a limit to the number of signals they can receive

(b) 26. Overall activation is increased by an _____ connection which contributes positive activation values.

   (a) an inhibitory
   (b) an excitatory
   (c) an input
   (d) an output

(a) 27. Overall activation is decreased by an _____ connection which contributes negative activation values.

   (a) an inhibitory
   (b) an excitatory
   (c) an input
   (d) an output

(b) 28. The Hebbian Learning Procedure is _____.

   (a) indefinite
   (b) limited
   (c) able to acquire correlated information
   (d) able to learn through error correction

(a) 29. In calculating changes in weights, how does the Delta procedure differ from the Hebb procedure?

   (a) the presence of the error term
   (b) the presence of the learning parameter
   (c) the absence of the error term
   (d) the absence of the learning parameter

(d) 30. Which of the following is an example of the double inflection response in learning the past tense of English verbs?

- (a) dripping
- (b) dropped
- (c) dripped
- (d) dripted

(a) 31. According to Hebb,

- (a) each memory, thought, sensation, and feeling is based on the activity pattern in a neural circuit.
- (b) thoughts are based on the activity pattern of a neural circuit, but memories are not.
- (c) no basis can be found for emotion in the brain.
- (d) memories are based on the activity pattern of a neural circuit, but thoughts are not.

(d) 32. The Delta procedure is capable of learning entire categories of input patterns and output patterns. You have learned a category when

- (a) a category can never be learned.
- (b) you respond correctly only to previously encountered stimuli that belong to the same category.
- (c) you do not generalize similar stimuli.
- (d) you respond correctly to novel stimuli that belong to the same category.

(d) 33. Information processing in computers is often compared to brain functions. Interestingly, computer chips process information _____ than neurons, and organisms recognize objects in the environment _____.

- (a) slower, faster
- (b) faster, at the same speed
- (c) slower, at the same speed
- (d) faster, faster

(d) 34. Connectionist models are well suited for situations where several conditions must be met at the same time in order to recognize an object or carry out an act. _____ is the term for interpreting and acting on several items of information simultaneously.

- (a) parallel processing
- (b) Delta learning
- (c) Hebbian learning
- (d) Constraint satisfaction

(c) 35. Neural networks consist of simple processing units, the cells or neurons. The neurons are connected through links that carry

    (a) inhibitory but not excitatory information
    (b) excitatory but not inhibitory information
    (c) both inhibitory and excitatory information
    (d) sensory data

(c) 36. Three-layer networks include input, output, and hidden units. Which of the following statements about these units is correct?

    (a) Both input and hidden units receive stimuli from the environment
    (b) Input units receive stimuli from the environment; both output and hidden units produce outcomes.
    (c) Both input and output, but not hidden units communicate with the environment.
    (d) Input, output, and hidden units communicate with the environment.

(d) 37. A neural net is a computer simulation of a circuit of neurons. Neural nets consist of

    (a) small units known as axons
    (b) weights that determine the strength of the connection
    (c) connections between neurons
    (d) both b and c

(b) 38. In a biological neuron the activation traveling between neurons is modulated at the synapse. By comparison, in neural network models such modulation is expressed by the multiplication of a weight by

    (a) another weight
    (b) an activation level
    (c) the output
    (d) the input

(c) 39. Researchers have arrived at a set of generalizations about neural networks. Which of the following statements is not a true generalization?

    (a) Activation spreads in parallel from the input units to the output unit(s).
    (b) Neurons accept input regardless of modality and source.
    (c) Details of the input signals are remembered after the aggregated output activation is determined.
    (d) Every unit in the system calculates an output except for the input neurons.

(c) 40. Collins and Quillian developed a semantic network where each node stores only one concept. This network is an example of

    (a) differentiated representation
    (b) distributed representation
    (c) localized representation
    (d) individual representation

(d) 41. Theorists have devised different means of representing information, each with its own properties. An advantage of _____ representation, for example, is that more items can be stored relative to the number of units than in a _____ storage system.

    (a) differentiated, individual
    (b) individual, differentiated
    (c) localized, distributed
    (d) distributed, localized

(c) 42. Please calculate the values missing in the following matrix

	INPUT				OUTPUT	
	1	-1	x	1		
WEIGHTS		-.25	y	.25	-.25	
PRODUCTS		z	-.25	0	-.25	-.75

    (a) x=-.25, y=+.25, z=+.25
    (b) x=0, y=-.25, z=-.25
    (c) x=0, y=+.25, z=-.25
    (d) x=-1, y=+.25, z=-.25

(b) 43. Because retrieval from neural networks is based both on full and partial input, degraded inputs may serve as retrieval probes as well. Which of the following statements can not be supported by this view?

    (a) Degraded input is a kind of partial input, even if there are some infelicities.
    (b) Memories must be retrieved through a specific prompt.
    (c) Human memory is extremely flexible.
    (d) We are able to recall "dog" with such verbal cues as "it barks" or "it wags its tail."

(b) 44. A matrix is an array of values that transforms the elements of an input vector to produce an output vector. This means that two different vectors, pushed through the same matrix, will

    (a) not produce an output
    (b) give different outputs
    (c) both produce outputs like the initial vector
    (d) both produce outputs like the most recent vector

(c) 45. According to different learning rules, the weights in neural nets change in different ways. In order to calculate weight changes according to the Hebb rule one

    (a) adds the input activation, the target activation, and the learning rate parameter
    (b) adds the input activation to the product of the target activation and the learning rate parameter
    (c) multiplies the input activation, the target activation, and the learning rate parameter
    (d) multiplies the input activation by the target activation and than adds the learning rate parameter

(a) 46. According to the Hebb rule, a weight is strengthened when two connected neurons are activated at the same time. The increase _____ the degree of activation of the two neurons. High activation levels produce _____ in the connection strength than low levels of activation

    (a) depends on, a greater increase
    (b) depends on, a greater decreases
    (c) depends on, a smaller increase
    (d) is independent of, the same change

(d) 47. The Delta and Hebb rules, and learning through backpropagation are three important procedures for the training of neural networks. The Hebbian learning procedure overcomes the limits of

    (a) Delta learning procedure
    (b) learning through backpropagation
    (c) both a and b
    (d) none of the above

(c) 48. One of the most interesting applications of Delta learning in cognitive psychology has been the simulation of acquiring linguistic regularities and exceptions, including the past tense of English verbs. What is the correct order in which the tense is acquired?

    (a) past tense of regular verbs, past tense of irregular, past tense of irregular
    (b) present tense of irregular verbs, past tense of irregular, past tense of regular
    (c) past tense of irregular verbs, past tense of regular, past tense of irregular
    (d) present tense of regular verbs, past tense of regular, present tense irregular

(a) 49. Rescorla and Wagner, discovered the Delta rule in the context of animal learning. According to the Rescorla- Wagner rule, an unexpected, weak stimulus will _____ if it is paired with reinforcement.

    (a) become stronger
    (b) go undetected
    (c) be unaffected
    (d) become even weaker

(b) 50. Patterns like the XOR pattern described in chapter 6 are not linearly separable and thus cause problems for Delta learning. Rumelhart, Hinton, and Williams (1986) discovered that patterns like XOR

- (a) cannot be learned by neural networks
- (b) can only be learned by the generalized Delta rule with the aid of hidden units
- (c) work the same as AND and OR patterns and thus causes problems
- (d) always produce an output of 0 and thus pose difficulties for Delta learning

(b) 51. Backpropagation learning includes several new features as compared to Delta learning. Which of these features is not used in back propagation learning

- (a) the logistic function
- (b) a two-layer network
- (c) backward activation
- (d) forward activation

(d) 52. In general, backpropagation learning is useful whenever an input must be transformed into an output that includes both regularities and exceptions. Which of these statements is an example of where backpropagation would be useful?

- (a) control of robot movements
- (b) interpret X-rays to detect symptoms of diseases
- (c) simulate the actions of a fighter pilot
- (d) all of the above

(b) 53. Recurrent networks are designed to capture relations between successive outputs of the network. This is possible

- (a) because recurrent networks only deal with previous inputs and outputs
- (b) due to the hidden units that feed their outputs back to themselves
- (c) as a result of the increased numbers of input and output vectors
- (d) because recurrent networks do not rely on previous inputs and outputs

(a) 54. Although neural networks have been largely praised, some criticisms have been raised as well. Which of these is not a criticism of neural networks?

- (a) Neural networks are frequently unsuccessful in simulating diverse data in cognition.
- (b) It is not clear that there are backpropagation pathways in the brain.
- (c) The programmer has great latitude in shaping the processing assumptions of the simulation.
- (d) Learning is too slow in neural networks.

(a) 55. The following matrix shows input activations, output activations, and weights. Please select the most appropriate statement.

```
     -1    +1
     .5    x      -.8
     y    -.3     +5
```

(a) x=-.3, y=-.8
(b) x=+.3, y=+.8
(c) x and y represent input
(d) both a and c are correct

(b) 56. Please calculate the output in the following matrix

```
  +1    +1    -1    +1

 -.25  +.25  -.25  +.25      w
 +.25  +.25  +.25  -.25      x
 -.25  -.25  +.25  +.25      y
 +.25  -.25  -.25  +.25      z
```

(a) w=+1 x=+1 y=+1 z=+1
(b) w=+.5 x=0   y=-.5 z=+.5
(c) w= 0 x=+.5 y=0   z=0
(d) output = +.5

CHAPTER 7

(a) 1. The following term refers to changes in behavior and knowledge through experience.

(a) learning
(b) memory
(c) conditioning
(d) habituation

(c) 2. When two events occur at the same time, we tend to connect them in our mind. This is the basis for learning by

(a) habituation
(b) instrumental conditioning
(c) contiguity
(d) sensitization

(c) 3. The "Law of Effect" was formulated by

    (a) Pavlov
    (b) Ebbinghaus
    (c) Thorndike
    (d) Hume

(b) 4. Research on animal and human learning

    (a) was based on the same theories but the methods were different
    (b) employed different experimental paradigms and terminologies
    (c) arrived at similar conclusions about the nature of reinforcement
    (d) concluded that stimulus generalization was a function of response strength

(a) 5. Animal learning researchers focused on

    (a) the acquisition of responses
    (b) retention of responses over time
    (c) interference
    (d) all of the above

(b) 6. Human learning researchers focused on

    (a) the acquisition of responses
    (b) retention of responses over time
    (c) classical learning theory
    (d) all of the above

(d) 7. Both classical learning theorists and memory researchers

    (a) had behaviorist views
    (b) were interested in the functional relations between stimuli and responses
    (c) were associationist theorists
    (d) all of the above

(a) 8. The link with animal learning research was severed when memory researchers in the 1960s

    (a) adopted the information processing approach
    (b) discovered the computer metaphor for learning
    (c) adopted a computer model of the stimulus-response framework
    (d) became interested in cognitive science

(b) 9. Animal learning theories have problems in investigating

    (a) functional relations between stimuli and responses
    (b) symbolic processing
    (c) associationism

(d) computer models

(c) 10. The following approach suggests that complex knowledge and performance is the result of elementary associations between simple units

    (a) stimulus-response approach
    (b) associationist approach
    (c) connectionist approach
    (d) information processing approach

(d) 11. Symbol-processing theories of cognition

    (a) are an extension of classical learning theories
    (b) are incompatible with classical learning theories
    (c) represent a special class of connectionist models
    (d) none of the above

(a) 12. According to symbolic processing theories, procedural knowledge is

    (a) rule based
    (b) innate
    (c) a result of conditioning
    (d) all of the above

(b) 13. Investigating the digestive system in dogs, Pavlov discovered that dogs were salivating well before receiving food. He called this the

    (a) unconditioned response
    (b) conditioned response
    (c) reflexive response
    (d) incidental response

(b) 14. In classical conditioning, the experimenter arranges for the following sequence of events

    (a) US, CS
    (b) CS, US
    (c) CS, CR
    (d) US, CR

(c) 15. The classical conditioning paradigm described in Chapter 7 included the following temporal relation of CS and US

    (a) the CS precedes the US and is terminated at the US onset
    (b) the US and CS must be strictly simultaneous in order to maximize the learning rate
    (c) the CS precedes the US and is terminated at the US offset
    (d) none of the above

(a) 16. In classical conditioning, researchers observe the following relation of responses

    (a) the UR follows the CR
    (b) the CR follows the UR
    (c) the two responses are additive occurring simultaneously
    (d) depending on the reinforcement schedule, each of the above may occur

(c) 17. Acquired taste aversion is based on the association of a taste and becoming sick after being exposed to a toxic agent. Acquired taste aversion is an instance of

    (a) sensitization
    (b) discrimination
    (c) conditioning
    (d) generalization

(b) 18. According to the law of effect

    (a) extinction is the effect of fatigue
    (b) the probability of a response increases if it is repeatedly followed by reinforcement
    (c) the effect of conditioning is the strengthening of the association between CS and US
    (d) instrumental conditioning is more effective than classical conditioning

(a) 19. In the instrumental learning paradigm,

    (a) reinforcement is contingent on the organism's behavior
    (b) the organism's behavior is contingent on reinforcement
    (c) the response is contingent on the stimulus
    (d) none of the above

(a) 20. In classical conditioning, the conditioned stimulus and unconditioned stimulus

    (a) are paired independently of what the organism does
    (b) eventually elicit the same response
    (c) depend on the organism's behavior
    (d) are from the same stimulus continuum in order to demonstrate discrimination learning

(c) 21. Strengthening a response through repeated reinforcements is known as _____.

    (a) the associative phase
    (b) extinction
    (c) the acquisition phase
    (d) spontaneous recovery

(a) 22. The following typically involves responding to novel stimuli

    (a) extinction
    (b) stimulus generalization
    (c) the acquisition phase
    (d) spontaneous recovery

(b) 23. A _____ involves the presentation of two distinct CSs during acquisition: the CS+ which is reinforced and the CS- which is not.

    (a) concept learning experiment
    (b) discriminative training schedule
    (c) conditioning experiment
    (d) all of the above

(b) 24. The tendency to confuse two stimuli is known as

    (a) discrimination
    (b) stimulus generalization
    (c) extinction
    (d) spontaneous recovery

(a) 25. In _____ a subject learns that a certain set of stimuli are subsumed by one category.

    (a) concept learning
    (b) associative learning
    (c) procedural learning
    (d) none of the above

(c) 26. The critical feature that contributes to learning is not _____; it is _____.

    (a) the signal value of the CS; contiguity
    (b) the number of CS-US pairings; the intensity of the CS and US
    (c) contiguity; the signal value of the CS
    (d) none of the above

(b) 27. According to the Law of Effect, any event that _____ the likelihood of a response is a reinforcer.

    (a) decreases
    (b) increases
    (c) holds steady
    (d) modulates

(b) 28. The _____ states that for any pair of responses, the more probable one will reinforce the less probable one.

 (a) law of effect
 (b) probability-difference principle
 (c) contiguity theory
 (d) signal value theory

(a) 29. According to the classic view of learning theorists, there are only a few specific stimuli such as food and drink for which animals are willing to work; these are called

 (a) primary reinforcers
 (b) secondary reinforcers
 (c) critical reinforcers
 (d) reinforcers

(a) 30. The shaping method of increasing the occurrence of responses is known as _____ when it is used with human patients in clinical applications.

 (a) behavior modification
 (b) conditioning
 (c) response training
 (d) learning

(c) 31. One of the limitations of behavior modification is that people quickly learn to discriminate between

 (a) a CS and a US
 (b) a CR and a UR
 (c) the settings where a reinforcement schedule is valid
 (d) different classes of reinforcing events

(b) 32. A wide range of behaviors are learned and shaped through the organism's exposure to

 (a) experimental procedures
 (b) its natural habitat
 (c) CSs
 (d) all of the above

(a) 33. Whenever you get used to an environment, you

 (a) habituate to it
 (b) dishabituate to it
 (c) are sensitized to it
 (d) are primed

(c) 34. The following term refers to increases in responsiveness as a result of repeated application of the eliciting stimulus

- (a) habituation
- (b) dishabituation
- (c) sensitization
- (d) priming

(d) 35. When a stimulus is presented several times, the time it takes to recognize the stimulus decreases with each repetition. This is an example of

- (a) habituation
- (b) dishabituation
- (c) sensitization
- (d) priming

(b) 36. There can be no learning without

- (a) habituation
- (b) memory
- (c) conditioning
- (d) reinforcement

(a) 37. Please choose the two terms that best complete the following assertions. Learning researchers emphasize performance as a function of _____; Memory researchers emphasize performance as a function of _____.

- (a) the number of reinforcements; time
- (b) time; the number of reinforcements
- (c) habituation; priming
- (d) priming; sensitization

(b) 38. Ebbinghaus was aware that memories and meanings are confounded; something that is

- (a) habituated is remembered better
- (b) meaningful is remembered better
- (c) unique is remembered better
- (d) recognizable is remembered better

(a) 39. Ebbinghaus' experiments consisted of two phases; original learning and relearning. This _____ provided a measure of the durability of memory traces.

- (a) savings method
- (b) retention method
- (c) priming method
- (d) stimulus-response method

(c) 40. Much as in animal learning, early human memory research emphasized _____, not _____.

   (a) the relation between time and retention; the causes of forgetting
   (b) the causes of forgetting; the relation between time and retention
   (c) the functional relations governing retention; mental structures and processes
   (d) mental structures and processes; the functional relations governing retention

(a) 41. Thorndike (1911) developed

   (a) the operant conditioning procedure
   (b) classical conditioning
   (c) interference theory
   (d) the habituation procedure

(b) 42. McGeoch (1942) challenged Thorndike's view of retention and forgetting and proposed

   (a) the law of disuse
   (b) interference theory
   (c) an operant conditioning procedure
   (d) failure-of-retrieval theory

(b) 43. The following term means that new information blocks out some prior information.

   (a) interference
   (b) retroactive interference
   (c) proactive interference
   (d) trace interference

(c) 44. The effects of prior learning on later learning are referred to as

   (a) interference
   (b) retroactive interference
   (c) proactive interference
   (d) the law of disuse

(a) 45. According to the learning theories by Hebb, Pavlov, and others, which of the following conditions is sufficient to produce learning?

   (a) the association of the CS with the US
   (b) the association of the CS with the UR
   (c) the association of the US with the UR
   (d) the association of the CR with the CS

(d) 46. Which of the following theorists expressed the view that disuse could not account for forgetting?

    (a) Underwood
    (b) Bartlett
    (c) Thorndike
    (d) McGeoch

(d) 47. The bond between the early classical learning theorists and memory researchers is their behaviorist views. What is true for both groups?

    (a) no such bond exists
    (b) both were interested in the mental apparatus that mediates between observable events
    (c) both emphasized mental structures, processes and mechanisms
    (d) both were interested in the functional relations between stimuli and responses

(b) 48. In Pavlov's classical conditioning paradigm, the flow of saliva triggered by the presence of the meat is the

    (a) unconditioned stimulus
    (b) unconditioned response
    (c) conditioned stimulus
    (d) conditioned response

(d) 49. "The probability of a response increases if it is repeatedly followed by reinforcement." This defines which law?

    (a) The Law of Free Recall
    (b) The Law of Contiguity
    (c) The Law of Acquisition
    (d) The Law of Effect

(c) 50. The experiment in which children were observed in a room with both a candy dispenser and a pinball machine helped Premack formulate

    (a) The conformity principle that children will "prefer" to do what other children do, regardless of a previously indicated preference.
    (b) The preference principle that "children will do what they prefer, but not if it is contingent upon doing something else first."
    (c) The probability-difference principle that "for any pair of responses, the more probable one will reinforce the less probable one."
    (d) The reinforcement principle that the same activities serve as reinforcement for everyone.

(d) 51. When a stimulus is presented to people several times, the time to recognize the stimulus decreases with each repetition. This is known as

    (a) behavior modification
    (b) desensitization
    (c) habituation
    (d) priming

(b) 52. In studies on the Rescorla-Wagner theory the conditioned stimulus is a reliable predictor of the unconditioned stimulus in the following condition.

    (a) free-US
    (b) contingent
    (c) relative
    (d) cue value

(d) 53. Using the savings method, Ebbinghaus learned and relearned sets of nonsense syllables under different retention intervals. Accordingly the savings after 30 minutes were ____% and the savings after 48 hours were ____%.

    (a) 10; 50
    (b) 50; 50
    (c) 100:25
    (d) 50:25

(a) 54. In the "noisy water" demonstration, rats drink normal water although it was previously associated by a loud noise with sickness. The point of this experiment was to show that

    (a) learning is constrained by the disposition of the organism
    (b) taste aversion depends on the taste of food
    (c) a rat can learn a wide range of associations
    (d) Thorndike was correct about the generalization of the laws of learning

(a) 55. The Ebbinghaus and Bartlett traditions had which of the following in common?

    (a) both studied retention over the long term
    (b) both used nonsense syllables in their research
    (c) both approached the information-processing approach to memory
    (d) both were associationists

(d) 56. Atkinson and Shiffrin's (1968) model of memory storage proposes _____ to describe the subject's mental activities.

    (a) algorithmic processes
    (b) search processes
    (c) rehearsal processes
    (d) control processes

(b) 57. According to Craik and Tulving (1975), it is _____, not _____ that determines memory strength.

   (a) maintenance rehearsal; elaborative rehearsal
   (b) elaborative rehearsal; maintenance rehearsal
   (c) elaborative rehearsal; repetitive rehearsal
   (d) repetitive rehearsal; associative rehearsal

(c) 58. When something is forgotten as a result of later interpolated learning, _____ has occurred.

   (a) proactive interference
   (b) retrieval failure
   (c) retroactive interference
   (d) recall interference

(c) 59. Cancer patients have a negative associative reaction to food eaten prior to chemotherapy. This illustrate a maladaptive acquired taste aversion response, which is:

   (a) an unconditioned response
   (b) due to the *Law of Effect*
   (c) adaptively used to avoid toxins
   (d) a cause of dehydration in the patient

(d) 60. Response patterns in acquisition and extinction phases of a typical learning experiment would be graphed as follows (circle the correct graph):

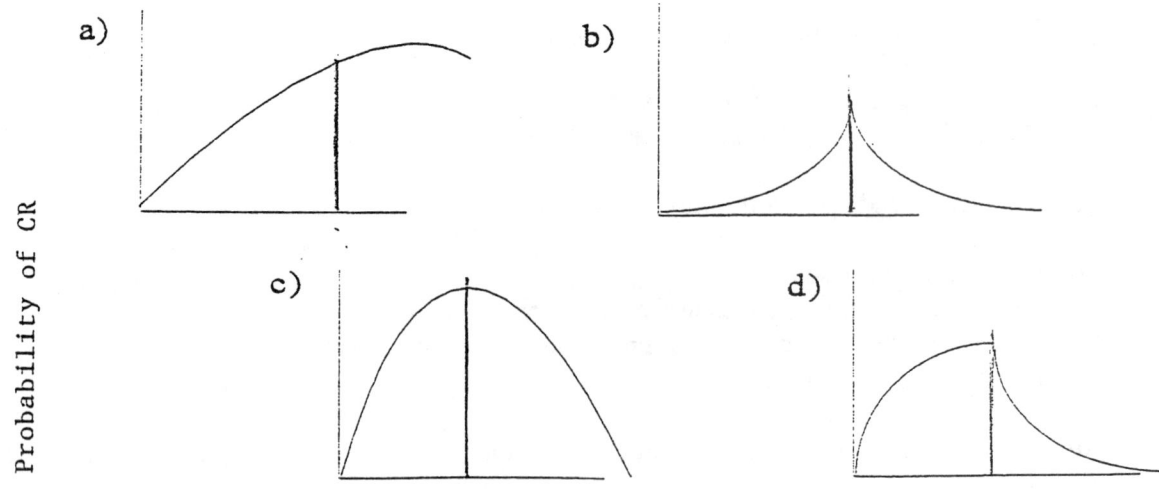

(d) 61. Assume that an experimenter reads three letters to you, and then asks you to count backwards by threes starting with 59. After 9 seconds you are asked to recall the three numbers. The researcher is testing what type of interference:

- (a) interactive interference
- (b) proactive interference
- (c) disuse
- (d) retroactive interference

(b) 62. When we recall unfamiliar information or situations found in a story, we recall or replace it with words or terms that we are familiar with. This exemplifies Bartlett's knowledge structures called:

- (a) coherent form
- (b) schema
- (c) proactive memory
- (d) pure memory

(d) 63. The effect of rehearsal of information is to prevent decay in a short-term trace, but it can also lead to:

- (a) free-recall
- (b) forgetting
- (c) acoustic confusion
- (d) transfer to long-term store

CHAPTER 8

(d) 1. Damage to the frontal lobes and the resulting performance decrement in a dual-task paradigm, as observed by Baddeley and Hitch (1994) in some Alzheimer's patients, suggest that this area serves as

- (a) information storage
- (b) the visuospatial sketchpad
- (c) the phonological loop
- (d) the central executive

(c) 2. According to Ericsson and Kintsch (1995) larger capacity, more resistant traces, and ready access to information are all attributes of:

- (a) concentration
- (b) short-term working memory
- (c) long-term working memory
- (d) chunking

(a) 3. Completion of tasks like the Wisconsin Card Sorting Test, which requires a pattern of constant shifting of criteria in sorting, are considered to require the:

    (a) central executive
    (b) temporal lobes
    (c) Broca's area
    (d) manual dexterity

(b) 4. Ericsson and Kintsch (1995) define two types of working memory; (1) a general processor for familiar as well as unfamiliar information and (2) a domain specific processor. These are referred to by the terms:

    (a) memory capacities
    (b) (1) short-term working memory & (2) long-term working memory
    (c) network models
    (d) (1) long-term working memory & (2) short-term working memory

(d) 5. If the mind worked in the most efficient pattern possible, would you expect it to use an _____ or a _____, as defined in Sternberg's serial search with digits, and which method was used?

    (a) self-terminating search, self-terminating search
    (b) exhaustive search, self-terminating search
    (c) both methods take equal time
    (d) self-terminating search, exhaustive search

(c) 6. A novel approach to interfering with working memory was used by Fuster (1995), where he reduced retention of colors in a delayed-response task by the simple procedure of:

    (a) elevating the level of neuron activity
    (b) single cell activation
    (c) cooling cortical regions
    (d) angular separation

(c) 7. Working memory is the principal processor of human cognition. Theories of working memory evolved from processing accounts of

    (a) sensory memory
    (b) long-term memory
    (c) short-term memory
    (d) central processor

(c) 8. According to traditional information processing theories, short-term memory was viewed as

    (a) the principal processor of cognition
    (b) a highly active processor
    (c) a relatively passive storage medium

(d) the mechanism of information retrieval

(a) 9. In Anderson's Act* Theory, working memory is the processor in which matching of the following entities takes place

   (a) productions; facts and goals
   (b) prototypes; features
   (c) feature; prototypes
   (d) none of the above

(b) 10. Baddeley's multi-component model of working memory includes

   (a) declarative, procedural, and analogical components
   (b) phonological, visuo-spatial, and control components
   (c) phonological, procedural, and analogical components
   (d) imagery, buffering, and control components

(b) 11. The following operation is a phonological process that involves the auditory and articulatory system.

   (a) comprehension
   (b) rehearsal
   (c) transformation
   (d) suppression

(a) 12. If you interfere with rehearsal by having a subject repeat an otherwise easy word, retention of target materials decreases even if the information is presented visually. This is known as the

   (a) phonological suppression effect
   (b) phonological confusion effect
   (c) verbal loop effect
   (d) verbal interference effect

(d) 13. The span of working memory is related to the number of phonemes to be memorized. This is known as the

   (a) phonological suppression effect
   (b) phonological confusion effect
   (c) verbal loop effect
   (d) word-length effect

(b) 14. Baddeley's "sketch pad" component of working memory includes processing of the following

   (a) verbal communication
   (b) visual imagery
   (c) phonological processing
   (d) allocates resources

(a) 15. In Brooks'(1968) interference experiments, saying "yes" and "no" interfered more with

    (a) remembering sentences than with mentally tracing a block letter
    (b) mentally tracing a block letter than with remembering sentences
    (c) mental tracing a block letter than with imaging it
    (d) with imaging a sentence than with recalling it

(c) 16. Baddeley's multi-component model of working memory includes codes for the following types of information in working memory

    (a) phonological, visual, semantic
    (b) phonological, abstract, semantic
    (c) visual, spatial, phonological
    (d) procedural, declarative, abstract

(a) 17. According to Baddeley's multi-component model of working memory the central executive

    (a) allocates resources
    (b) stores information
    (c) processes modality-specific information
    (d) does all of the above

(b) 18. The term "working memory" was first introduced in the context of research on

    (a) human memory
    (b) problem solving
    (c) comprehension
    (d) mental search and comparison

(c) 19. In the Tower of Hanoi problem, the person must move a set of disks from one peg to another while observing a set of constraints. This puzzle becomes more difficult as

    (a) new constraints are added to the problem
    (b) the interference between constraints and disk moves increases
    (c) more subgoals must be remembered
    (d) more pegs are added

(d) 20. In Daneman's span test the subject is given

    (a) a set of digits to add and asked to memorize the sums
    (b) a set of digits and asked to memorize them
    (c) a set of words, asked to form sentences, and to remember them
    (d) a set of sentences and asked to remember the final words

(b) 21. Daneman's span test requires the subject to

- (a) memorize digits and transform them
- (b) comprehend and store sentences
- (c) comprehend and transform sentences
- (d) comprehend sentences and memorize digits

(a) 22. In Posner and Rossman's experiment subjects were asked to

- (a) memorize digits and transform them
- (b) comprehend and store sentences
- (c) comprehend and transform sentences
- (d) comprehend sentences and memorize digits

(d) 23. In Sternberg's memory scanning task, Yes-responses are executed by x and No-responses are executed by y. Choose the appropriate pair of x and y

- (a) x: parallel search, y: serial search
- (b) x: self-terminating search, y: exhaustive search
- (c) x: serial search, y: exhaustive search
- (d) x: exhaustive search, y: exhaustive search

(c) 24. In the memory scanning task, typically the following results are observed

- (a) the slope of Yes-responses is steeper than that of No-responses
- (b) the slope of No-responses is steeper than that of Yes-responses
- (c) the slope of Yes-responses does not differ from that of No-responses
- (d) the slope of Yes-responses and No-responses depends on the trade-off conditions

(c) 25. Processing in working memory involves a trade-off between operations. Choose the best fitting pair of processes that compete for working-memory resources.

- (a) search; comprehension
- (b) search; transformation
- (c) storage; computation
- (d) all of the above

(d) 26. Research has shown that individuals have a hard time discriminating among the sound of the letters T, V, C, and D. This effect is known as

- (a) the Phonological Suppression Effect
- (b) the Verbal Loop Effect
- (c) the Word-Length Effect
- (d) the Phonological Confusion Effect

(c) 27. The memory scanning task may engage different types of search processes, including a serial search. In a serial search, the target digit is

    (a) compared with the reaction rate of the target
    (b) compared with the search time of the target
    (c) compared sequentially with each of the digits in the memory set
    (d) compared simultaneously to each of the digits in the memory set

(b) 28. Combining items of information so as to use less memory capacity reflects the notion of

    (a) rehearsal
    (b) chunking
    (c) selectivity
    (d) encoding

(b) 29. Ericsson and Polson studied the memory of a waiter, JC. JC was able to memorize up to 20 different orders without writing them down. The point of this experiment was that

    (a) one remembers something by mapping the new information in terms of discrimination with something else in long term memory
    (b) one remembers something by mapping the new information in terms of familiar information in long term memory
    (c) one remembers something immediately after perceiving the new information
    (d) one remembers something by mapping the new information in terms of generalizing to other information in long term memory

(a) 30. Just and Carpenter devised an experiment to track the mental rotation process by incorporating 3-D cubelike figures. In doing so, they distinguished between all of the following eye movement patterns except

    (a) resolution stage
    (b) comparison phase
    (c) confirmation stage
    (d) search stage

(b) 31. Working memory storage capacity limits

    (a) are best captured by five chunks (items) of information
    (b) can be expanded by practicing memorization of specific content
    (c) can be expanded only at the expense of long-term memory capacity
    (d) can be expanded only in exceptional individuals

(d) 32. Which of the following is true of the Central Executive component of Baddeley's theory?

    (a) schedules deliberate processes in working memory
    (b) governs automatic processes in working memory
    (c) it is primarily a storage space

(d) it is the processor that controls the operations of working memory

(d) 33. Which component in Baddeley's theory is primarily implicated in remembering information?

(a) visuo-spatial sketch pad
(b) the central executive
(c) the audio-visual executive
(d) the phonological component

(c) 34. Working memory contains

(a) conscious information
(b) only unconscious information
(c) both conscious and unconscious information
(d) semantic information

(c) 35. With which of the following statements would Sternberg agree?

(a) Yes-responses are never the result of self-terminating searches.
(b) No-responses necessarily involve a self-terminating search.
(c) Search involves a mental target and a mental search set.
(d) No more than two cognitive operations can take place concurrently.

(d) 36. According to Baddeley, which of the following does the Central Executive do?

(a) stores information
(b) processes modality-specific operation
(c) acts on phonological stimuli
(d) governs attentional and automatic processes

(b) 37. Cognitive psychologists have proposed several models of memory search, including the self-terminating search. In a self-terminating search

(a) the target digit is compared to every digit in the memory set before search is terminated
(b) when a match between target and a memorized digit is found, the search is terminated
(c) the target digit is compared simultaneously to each memorized digit before the search is terminated
(d) the target digit is compared sequentially to each digit in the memory set

(d) 38. The working memory in a production system communicates with

(a) declarative memory
(b) production memory
(c) the environment
(d) all of the above

(a) 39. Just and Carpenter (1976) recorded eye movement patterns which reflected the mind's current work. This type of research is based on

    (a) the eye-mind assumption
    (b) the eye tracking technique
    (c) a mental image transformation
    (d) eye fixations

(b) 40. Just and Carpenter (1976) recorded eye fixation patterns of subjects participating in a mental rotation task. According to these researchers, the comparison phase is the phase in which

    (a) subjects scan two comparison objects unsystematically
    (b) subjects fixate eyes on corresponding parts of figures
    (c) subject fixates eyes on the center of each figure and shifts toward the ends
    (d) subjects fixate on different parts of same object

(b) 41. According to Hunt (1978), general intelligence is correlated with the

    (a) length of memory span
    (b) speed of working memory processes
    (c) extent of phonological memory skills
    (d) digit span capacity

(c) 42. Frontal Lobe Syndrome has the following symptoms except

    (a) high level of distraction
    (b) attention to extraneous environmental stimuli
    (c) inappropriate eye fixation patterns
    (d) inability to plan and organize

(b) 43. Posner and Rossman (1965) demonstrated that the work load in working memory competes with

    (a) storage capacity in long-term memory
    (b) storage capacity in working memory
    (c) comprehension of material given
    (d) storage capacity in declarative memory

(d) 44. A phonological process used to remember new information which involves the auditory or articulatory system is known as

    (a) word-length effect
    (b) inner voice
    (c) phonological search effect
    (d) none of the above

(a) 45. Brooks (1986) conducted a study using images in visual and auditory modalities. When the image and the response involved the same modality,

    (a) responses were difficult
    (b) there was no interference
    (c) no response was made
    (d) none of the above

(c) 46. In a parallel search, reaction times

    (a) increase with the size of the memory set
    (b) decrease with the size of the memory set
    (c) do not vary with the size of the memory set
    (d) are the same as in a serial search

(a) 47. The PET scan detects changes in the flow of blood in cerebral regions. Posner and colleagues (1988) found that when a subject was reading a list of nouns, blood flow increased

    (a) in the visual processing area
    (b) in the auditory processing area
    (c) in both the visual and auditory processing areas
    (d) in the frontal lobe

(d) 48. The limit to the number of productions and propositions held in working memory is guided by the following processes except by

    (a) decay processes
    (b) refractoriness
    (c) communication with declarative memory and the environment
    (d) self-terminating search

(c) 49. Gathercole and Baddeley (1990) examined children with low verbal scores. They found that

    (a) verbal intelligence was independent of nonverbal intelligence
    (b) verbal scores were correlated with quantitative scores
    (c) their subjects had poor phonological memory skills
    (d) their subjects exhibited greater PET-activity during reading

CHAPTER 9

(c) 1. Cognitive neuroscientists consider the possibility structures of the brain are implicated in different memory functions. According to Tulving and colleagues (1994) retrieval of episodic and semantic memory are supported by the

    (a) right and left hippocampus
    (b) right and left occipital lobes
    (c) right and left prefrontal lobes
    (d) right and left ventricle

(a) 2. Retrieval of information from memory is a function of learning and testing. Retrieval is facilitated when learning and testing are in the same state or conditions. So for an exam, overall retention of material, would be accomplished best by studying:

    (a) sober in the exam room
    (b) sober in your dorm
    (c) drunk in the library
    (d) drunk in the exam room

(d) 3. In free recall of word lists, providing a partial list of words as a cues does not improve recall over a non-cued control group. The SAM model accounts for this partial list cuing effect by hypothesizing that:

    (a) only familiar words are provided
    (b) test anxiety interferes
    (c) only self-generated cues are useful
    (d) cues provided by the experimenter bias the sampling process to the exclusion of self-generated cues

(b) 4. The *fuzzy trace theory* accounts for false memory, such as adding the recall of the non-presented word *sun*, to a list of words like *beach, summer, hot, burn*, by theorizing that learners represent (1) series of events verbatim, and (2) that

    (a) they lose track of other words
    (b) they generate theme representation
    (c) they are unlikely to remember additional information
    (d) these memories cause interference

(c) 5. Reber (1993) created an artificial grammar using letters and certain transition rules as the base. He found that grammatical letter strings were recalled better than ungrammatical ones, even when subjects were unaware of the difference. He concluded that the rules of grammar were learned:

    (a) over long years of study
    (b) explicitly and consciously
    (c) implicitly without conscious awareness
    (d) only for test situations

(a) 6. Taking an evolutionary perspective, Reber (1993) felt that the persistence of implicit learning and memory in impaired populations indicated that:

    (a) it is more robust and phylogenetically prior to explicit learning
    (b) abstract knowledge is easily disrupted
    (c) explicit learning separates us from animals
    (d) it has a more complex superstructure

(b) 7. Which of the following is not one of the three major stages in the life of a memory representation?

    (a) encoding
    (b) activation
    (c) storage
    (d) retrieval

(a) 8. At any given time, most of our stored representations are

    (a) inactive
    (b) active
    (c) abstract
    (d) episodic

(a) 9. According to Chapter 9, memory has many dimensions, including the following pair

    (a) memory strength and state of activation
    (b) memory strength and storage strength
    (c) retrieval availability and state of activation
    (d) retrieval availability and storage strength

(c) 10. The state of activation of a representation is temporary, because

    (a) it depends on the memory strength of the representation
    (b) it is equal to the memory strength of the representation
    (c) it is independent of the memory strength of the representation
    (d) it is related to the durability of the representation

(a) 11. The level of activation of a representation refers to its

    (a) availability
    (b) durability
    (c) strength
    (d) all of the above

(c) 12. The most active information in memory is known as

   (a) long-term memory
   (b) short-term memory
   (c) working memory
   (d) rehearsal memory

(c) 13. Cognitive psychologists distinguish between the following types of memory

   (a) procedural vs. abstract
   (b) short-term vs. working
   (c) semantic vs. episodic
   (d) declarative vs. episodic

(d) 14. The following type of knowledge includes motor and cognitive skills

   (a) semantic
   (b) episodic
   (c) declarative
   (d) procedural

(c) 15. The following kind of knowledge contains information about the physical and social environment

   (a) semantic
   (b) episodic
   (c) declarative
   (d) procedural

(b) 16. When we remember both the factual content and the circumstances of acquiring the information we refer to the following kind of memory

   (a) semantic
   (b) episodic
   (c) declarative
   (d) procedural

(a) 17. List learning is studied using two major methods. They are

   (a) recall and recognition
   (b) encoding and retention
   (c) retrieval and context
   (d) cue and context

(b) 18. The retention paradigm, in which the person receives a list of items and reproduces it, is called

    (a) recognition
    (b) recall
    (c) cued retention
    (d) all of the above

(a) 19. When the subject identifies an "old" item as "new" in recognition testing the following response type results

    (a) miss
    (b) hit
    (c) false alarm
    (d) correct rejection

(d) 20. Retention depends on the following factors

    (a) retention interval and study time
    (b) list length and encoding context
    (c) position of items in the list and depth of processing
    (d) all of the above

(b) 21. In general, retention improves as

    (a) retention interval increases
    (b) study time increases
    (c) serial position decreases
    (d) encoding specificity decreases

(b) 22. It is usually easier to

    (a) recall an item than to recognize it
    (b) recognize an item than to recall it
    (c) retrieve an item than to retain it
    (d) retain an item than to encode it

(a) 23. Based on research, we can conclude that it is better to _____ rather than _____.

    (a) distribute practice over several sessions; study the same amount in a single session
    (b) study in a single session; distribute the same amount over several sessions
    (c) study in a familiar place; study where the test will be given
    (d) memorize the physical attributes of items; memorize items in their context

(c) 24. It is easier to access a representation when the context at retrieval is similar to the context during learning. This is known as

    (a) the retrieval structure effect
    (b) distinctive cue effect
    (c) encoding specificity effect
    (d) context dependent retrieval

(d) 25. Forgetting is based on

    (a) weakening of the memory trace due to decay
    (b) weakening of the memory trace due to interference
    (c) retrieval failure
    (d) all of the above

(a) 26. According to Tulving, the two conditions of remembering information successfully are

    (a) the existence of a trace and something to remind us of it
    (b) the existence of a trace and adequate memory strength
    (c) adequate memory strength and level of activation
    (d) correct encoding and enduring storage of the memory trace

(c) 27. Words that occur frequently in the English language are

    (a) relatively well recognized
    (b) relatively poorly encoded
    (c) relatively poorly recognized
    (d) none of the above

(c) 28. Recognition performance of items is ranked as follows

    (a) 1. organized items, 2. randomized items
    (b) 1. frequently occurring words; 2. infrequent words
    (c) 1. rare words; 2. frequent words
    (d) 1. stored words; 2. encoded words

(c) 29. The major frameworks of memory assume that

    (a) the memory for target items is independent of the memory of other items learned
    (b) to-be-learned materials are associated with context during storage
    (c) each item to-be-remembered has some pre-experimental memory strength
    (d) all of the above

(d) 30. The following generalizations describe performance in a recognition test

    (a) when a word is presented during the study phase, its memory strength is temporarily boosted
    (b) subjects base their decision about whether an item in a recognition test is "old" or "new" on its familiarity
    (c) if the familiarity value of the criterion is greater than the stimulus strength, the subject judges the item as "old"
    (d) a and b above

(d) 31. The representations of items in episodic memory have many features which include

    (a) they carry information about the context in which the item was learned
    (b) they carry information about other items in the list
    (c) they carry information about the item itself
    (d) all of the above

(a) 32. In SAM, the following term refers to the relatedness among the learned items, distractor items, and the associations of the items to the experimental context.

    (a) retrieval structure
    (b) contextual retrieval
    (c) encoding specificity
    (d) context structure

(c) 33. Which of the following is not a factor that influences the memory strength of a representation as a result of the experiment?

    (a) self-strength
    (b) context strength
    (c) association strength
    (d) inter-item strength

(a) 34. In the SAM model, the degree of association between an item and its memory representation is referred to as

    (a) self-strength
    (b) context strength
    (c) association strength
    (d) inter-item strength

(d) 35. In a memory experiment, context includes

    (a) the trial number
    (b) the list number
    (c) general context cues
    (d) all of the above

(c) 36. According to the SAM model, the familiarity of a list item is influenced by its relatedness to other items in the list. This reflects

   (a) context strength
   (b) association strength
   (c) inter-item strength
   (d) a and b above

(b) 37. In Raaijmakers and Shiffrin's SAM model, representations of items that are not presented during an experimental trial may be connected to the list items. This reflects

   (a) context strength
   (b) distractor strength
   (c) association strength
   (d) inter-item strength

(d) 38. According to Raaijmakers and Shiffrin's memory model, item strength values depend on _____ and _____.

   (a) the number of rehearsals; the depth of processing
   (b) pre-experimental familiarity; similarity between context cues during study and testing
   (c) retrieval structure; activation level of a cue
   (d) a and b above

(b) 39. The following type of memory refers to all of the general information that we acquire yet do not remember exactly where or when we learned it

   (a) episodic
   (b) semantic
   (c) explicit
   (d) implicit

(a) 40. According to Chapter 9, Anderson's ACT theory addresses all of the following ideas except

   (a) deep structure learning
   (b) list learning
   (c) sentence learning
   (d) memory of procedural skills

(d) 41. Long term memory is limited

   (a) as far as the amount of information concerned
   (b) as far as the complexity of information is concerned
   (c) as far as the duration is concerned
   (d) long term memory has no limits

(a) 42. Why is it difficult for you to remember a fact such as the capital of Nebraska, even though you memorized it in the fifth grade?

    (a) the fact has low memory strength
    (b) the activation level of the memory trace is too low
    (c) the fact has great memory strength
    (d) memory is dependent upon intelligence

(d) 43. Procedural Knowledge includes

    (a) skills we can easily verbalize
    (b) our knowledge of word meanings
    (c) information about the physical environment
    (d) motor skills

(b) 44. According to Raaijmakers and Shiffrin's theory, which of the following is not a factor that influences the memory strength of a representation as a result of the experiment?

    (a) self strength
    (b) temporary strength
    (c) context strength
    (d) distractor strength

(b) 45. According to the Raaijmakers and Shiffrin retrieval model, the memory strength of items is captured in a

    (a) dimensional structure
    (b) retrieval structure
    (c) representational structure
    (d) encoding structure

(b) 46. According to the Encoding Specificity Principle, recall is better in the condition in which

    (a) context cues are dropped between learning and testing
    (b) encoding and testing environments are the same
    (c) context cues are added between learning and testing
    (d) the memory trace is fully intact

(d) 47. We all know that we retain less when more time has lapsed since study. According to the Raaijmakers and Shiffrin retrieval framework, this occurs because

    (a) inter-item cues have changed more as the retention interval increases
    (b) self-strength cues have changed more as the retention interval increases
    (c) retention is affected by primacy and recency effects
    (d) context cues have changed more as the retention interval increases

(b) 48. When more information about a given concept is provided in a series of learning trials, activation spreads. As a result, its propagation through the network is slowed down. This is known as

    (a) category size effect
    (b) fan effect
    (c) assimilation effect
    (d) context cue interference

(c) 49. In a sentence recognition study, Bradshaw and Anderson (1982) manipulated the relatedness of elaborations to target items and compared their effectiveness on target recognition. Facts related to the target information improved retention by all of the following except

    (a) adding new retrieval paths
    (b) helping learners draw inferences
    (c) increasing connection strengths
    (d) helping learners reconstruct target facts

(d) 50. According to Linton (1982), which of the following influences the memorability of an event?

    (a) familiarity
    (b) importance
    (c) emotional value
    (d) distinctiveness

(c) 51. The Tip of the Tongue phenomenon results from the fact that

    (a) the encoding and recall contexts of items are different
    (b) the item is not sufficiently distinctive
    (c) memory representations contain features which may not be accessible
    (d) the person has failed to use a mnemonic technique to overcome memory deficit

(b) 52. Mnemonic techniques are effective because

    (a) they affect encoding specificity
    (b) they create a retrieval system in long-term memory
    (c) they bring together several features of a memory representation
    (d) they facilitate partial recall

(c) 53. Implicit and explicit memory performance differ on several dimensions. Which of the following is not an example of a dissociation effect?

    (a) developmental dissociation
    (b) drug-related dissociation
    (c) facilitative dissociation
    (d) clinical dissociation

(a) 54. Prior exposure to information facilitates subsequent performance in the word fragment completion task. This effect has been attributed to

    (a) implicit memory
    (b) explicit memory
    (c) dissociation
    (d) spreading activation

(a) 55. Anterograde amnesia involves

    (a) inability to acquire new episodic memory
    (b) inability to recall events prior to traumatic head injury
    (c) inability to exhibit implicit memory
    (d) inability to recall old long-term memories

(d) 56. Clinical memory deficits commonly affect

    (a) implicit memory
    (b) procedural skills
    (c) semantic memory
    (d) episodic memory

CHAPTER 10

(d) 1. Pinker (1994) used ERP patterns to show that an additional processing load is found in readers when they encounter a transformational trace. This indicates that:

    (a) reading is an automatic process
    (b) readers experience some difficulty with transformational traces in a sentence
    (c) early research was not sensitive enough to validate transformations
    (d) b & c

(b) 2. Translation systems, derived from principle-based grammars, are consistent with the connectionist approach and easier to use by the computer, because:

    (a) they are similar to rule-based translation systems
    (b) they are flexible and require one set of principles
    (c) require a different rule for each language
    (d) all of the above

(a) 3. On a spectrogram, the sound pattern of speech is displayed as energy bands at specific frequencies over a brief period of time. These energy bands are called:

    (a) formants
    (b) modulars
    (c) alveolars
    (d) phonemes

(c) 4. According to the reinforcement theory of language learning, parents and other adults correct the incorrect phrases used by a child. This theory is currently:

    (a) held to be the most likely acquisition method
    (b) used by language researchers
    (c) is too simplistic to teach complex knowledge like syntax
    (d) has been supported in studies of child/parent interaction

(b) 5. The view that linguistics describes the regularities of all languages is referred to as

    (a) the commonality theorem
    (b) the universality principle
    (c) language ethnocentrism
    (d) a & b above

(a) 6. The principal sources for linguistic research and theory is/are

    (a) sentence
    (b) word
    (c) phrase
    (d) all of the above

(a) 7. The constituent configuration most frequently found in the English language is

    (a) SVO
    (b) VSO
    (c) OVS
    (d) none of the above

(b) 8. The body of abstract knowledge that describes the word order in sentences is called

    (a) grammar
    (b) syntax
    (c) intuition
    (d) all of the above

(a) 9. According to Chomsky's early work, grammatically correct sequences of words are generated by

    (a) phrase structure rules
    (b) transformational rules
    (c) phrase structure trees
    (d) syntactic principles

(d) 10. Which of the following is not a syntactic category?

- (a) sentence
- (b) auxiliary verb
- (c) particle
- (d) phrase

(b) 11. The following is formally known as a terminal constituent; the application of rewrite rules is terminated when this item is encountered.

- (a) noun
- (b) word
- (c) object
- (d) verb

(a) 12. The following constituents define the hierarchical structure of a sentence

- (a) non-terminal
- (b) terminal
- (c) phrase
- (d) grammatical

(c) 13. The hierarchical structure of a sentence is the

- (a) phrase structure rule
- (b) surface form
- (c) phrase marker
- (d) deep structure

(b) 14. The underlined phrase in the sentence "Mary kicked the ball with blue dots" is expressed by the following rule

- (a) VP -> NP + PP
- (b) NP -> NP + PP
- (c) NP -> NP + ADJ + NP
- (d) none of the above

(c) 15. The grammatical sequence of words in a sentence is referred to as

- (a) phrase structure tree
- (b) deep structure
- (c) surface form
- (d) none of the above

(d) 16. According to Chomsky, the underlying meaning relationship of the sentence is expressed by

    (a) the semantic structure
    (b) the phrase marker
    (c) the phrase structure
    (d) the deep structure

(d) 17. The generative powers of simple phrase structure rules can be increased by

    (a) adding terminal elements
    (b) allowing optional categories
    (c) allowing category repetition
    (d) all of the above

(a) 18. The set of rules that generates grammatical sentences is known as

    (a) grammar
    (b) syntax
    (c) language
    (d) all of the above

(b) 19. A rule that is defined in terms of itself is called

    (a) a rewrite rule
    (b) recursive
    (c) phrase structure
    (d) a deep structure rule

(a) 20. According to Chomsky and his students, sentence ambiguities can be resolved by the implementation

    (a) of transformational rules
    (b) of phrase structure grammar
    (c) of syntactic principles
    (d) of a recursive grammar

(b) 21. A transformational rule takes a phrase marker generated by phrase structure rules as its input, and produces the following as its output.

    (a) deep structure
    (b) surface form
    (c) grammatical form
    (d) all of the above

(b) 22. A question transformation transforms the following type of sentences into a type of question.

    (a) ambiguous
    (b) active declarative
    (c) positive assertion
    (d) affirmative command

(b) 23. The conditions that permit use of the NP deletion rule include the following

    (a) the NP to be deleted is the logical object of the preceding NP
    (b) the NP to be deleted is identical to the preceding NP
    (c) the NP to be deleted was referred to in the previous constituent
    (d) the NP to be deleted is the subject of the deep structure

(d) 24. X can account for more regularities among English sentences than Y alone

    (a) X: the theta-criterion; Y: argument structure
    (b) X: argument structure; Y: the theta-criterion
    (c) X: phrase structure grammar; Y: transformational grammar
    (d) X: transformational grammar; Y: phrase structure grammar

(c) 25. The following generates word orders not found in English at all.

    (a) the universality principle
    (b) phrase structure grammar
    (c) transformational grammar
    (d) generative grammar

(b) 26. According to the complexity theory of comprehension, the _____ of a sentence should mirror the _____ process.

    (a) transformation; derivation
    (b) comprehension; derivation
    (c) generating process; transformation
    (d) none of the above

(d) 27. According to the complexity theory of comprehension

    (a) the more complex the sentence structure, the more difficult it is to comprehend
    (b) comprehension is accomplished by reversing the transformations used to derive the surface sentence
    (c) the more transformations used to derive the sentence, the more complex the sentence will be
    (d) all of the above

(c) 28. The complexity theory of comprehension predicts that _____ sentences could be interpreted faster than _____ sentences.

    (a) passive; active
    (b) complex; simple
    (c) active; passive
    (d) b & c above

(a) 29. A verb's argument structure refers to the _____.

    (a) set of noun phrases that the verb requires
    (b) set of verb phrases that the noun requires
    (c) set of prepositional phrases that the noun and verb require
    (d) all of the above

(d) 30. Which of the following is a verb subcategory

    (a) transitive
    (b) intransitive
    (c) predicate
    (d) a & b above

(d) 31. The theta-criterion stipulates that

    (a) every noun phrase must be an argument of a verb
    (b) every argument must be assigned to a verb
    (c) there can be no free-floating noun phrases
    (d) all of the above

(a) 32. The noun phrases of a sentence are specified by

    (a) verbs
    (b) nouns
    (c) syntactic rules
    (d) phrase structure rules

(c) 33. The clause "the girl hit the ball the wall" violates the theta-criterion because

    (a) the NP "the ball" has no argument
    (b) the verb "hit" allows no argument
    (c) the verb "hit" governs a NP and a PP
    (d) none of the above

(d) 34. The clause "the boy slept the couch" violates

    (a) transformational grammar
    (b) phrase structure grammar
    (c) syntactic principles
    (d) the theta-criterion

(a) 35. An argument structure refers to the set of _____ that the _____ requires.

    (a) noun phrases; verb
    (b) verb phrases; noun
    (c) prepositional phrases; noun
    (d) all of the above

(d) 36. Chapter 10 mentions several transformations including the particle-movement transformation. This rule moves the particle from the position right after the _____ to immediately after the _____.

    (a) subject; verb
    (b) verb; subject
    (c) object; verb
    (d) verb; object

(c) 37. Miller has estimated that an American high school student knows approximately the following number of words.

    (a) 20,000
    (b) 30,000
    (c) 40,000
    (d) 100,000

(b) 38. Which of the following is not an example of phrase structure rules or rewrite rules?

    (a) S--> NP + VP
    (b) VP--> ART + N
    (c) V--> hit,...
    (d) ART--> the, a,...

(c) 39. Transformational grammar is too powerful because

    (a) it forms sentences in less than 200 milliseconds
    (b) it can be generalized to different sentences
    (c) it can be used to generate word orders that are not found in English
    (d) none of the above

(c) 40. According to Susan Chollar (1989), dolphins, who have been dubbed our 'cognitive cousins', understand the meaning of

   (a) symbols
   (b) sentences
   (c) both of the above
   (d) none of the above

(d) 41. In light of Noam Chomsky's view of grammar, sentences are best represented as a

   (a) group of words
   (b) string of words
   (c) group of clauses
   (d) hierarchical structure

(a) 42. The science that investigates the knowledge necessary to interpret sentences, words, and sounds is

   (a) linguistics
   (b) logic
   (c) semantics
   (d) psycholinguistics

(d) 43. Linguists strive to describe language universally so that regularities of all languages are expressed. This is called the _____.

   (a) global view
   (b) global principle
   (c) universal view
   (d) universality principle

(a) 44. Linguists call a set of rules that generate grammatical sentences

   (a) grammar
   (b) phrase structure rules
   (c) lexicon
   (d) transformational rules

(c) 45. According to Chomsky's (1965) theory, the following are required to generate surface sentences.

   (a) phrase structure rules
   (b) transformational rules
   (c) both a and b
   (d) none of the above

(c) 46. The theory that states that the comprehension difficulty of a sentence reflects the generation of the sentence via transformational rules is the

    (a) mirror theory
    (b) derivational theory of generation
    (c) complexity theory of comprehension
    (d) transformational theory

(b) 47. Linguists have formulated a principle that expresses the relation between verbs and noun phrases. This principle is called

    (a) the linguistic principle
    (b) the theta-criterion
    (c) Berwick's principle
    (d) the recursion principle

(a) 48. According to Chapter 10, the correct propositional representation for the sentence "The butler is cooking supper for Mary" is

    (a) (cook, butler, supper, Mary)
    (b) (butler, cook, supper, Mary)
    (c) (Mary, butler, cook, supper)
    (d) (cook, supper, Mary, butler)

(b) 49. Propositions may also be used to represent non-linguistic information. How would the following visual scene be represented, according to Carpenter and Just (1975)?

    *

    +

    (a) (asterisk, above, plus)
    (b) (above, asterisk, plus)
    (c) (below, plus, asterisk)
    (d) (plus, below, asterisk)

(a) 50. Ratcliff and McKoon, in their study of propositions in language processes found that

    (a) people remember information in terms of propositional units
    (b) people remember information one word at a time
    (c) propositions interfere with memory
    (d) propositions predict reading performance

(c) 51. According to linguists and psycholinguists, which of the following is a type of mental dictionary which includes a word's morphological structure, its syntactic roles, and information about meaning?

    (a) morpheme structure
    (b) theta criterion
    (c) lexicon
    (d) semantic memory

(b) 52. There are _____ morphemes in the word "rework."

    (a) 1
    (b) 2
    (c) 3
    (d) 6

(d) 53. A sound that produces a difference in meaning is called a

    (a) morpheme
    (b) formant
    (c) agent
    (d) phoneme

(a) 54. Voiced phonemes are produced when the vocal chords vibrate as the air passes through them. Which of the following is not a voiced phoneme?

    (a) p
    (b) d
    (c) z
    (d) g

(b) 55. Which of the following is not an example of a voiceless phoneme?

    (a) t
    (b) v
    (c) f
    (d) s

(c) 56. Sounds produced by restricting the passage of air in the vocal tract are called

    (a) alveolar
    (b) voiceless
    (c) fricative
    (d) consonant

(c) 57. A word component that has a unique sound and also bears meaning is known as a

- (a) metaphor
- (b) simile
- (c) morpheme
- (d) phoneme

(a) 58. Adverbs, adjectives, nouns, and verbs are known as

- (a) content words
- (b) closed class words
- (c) function words
- (d) conjunctions

(a) 59. Our ability to pronounce words correctly is based on

- (a) phonological rules
- (b) semantic rules
- (c) morphological rules
- (d) syntactic rules

(b) 60. According to Noam Chomsky's view of grammar,

- (a) sentence structures are best represented in a string of words rather than a hierarchical structure
- (b) sentences are best represented in a hierarchical structure rather than a string of words
- (c) sentences are best represented in constituent phrases rather than a hierarchical structure
- (d) sentences are best represented in a hierarchical structure than in constituent phrases

(c) 61. According to Chomsky, the meaning of a sentence is expressed by the

- (a) phrase structure tree
- (b) phrase marker
- (c) deep structure
- (d) surface form

CHAPTER 11

(b) 1. The changing of a single letter at a time, from an initial word such as *time*, to produce others words like, *lime, dime, mime, etc.* creates a orthographic group of words that affects recognition time of the initial word. This is called

- (a) the search model
- (b) the neighborhood effect
- (c) a mental dictionary
- (d) a neural network

(c) 2. Assume a researcher presents a sequence of sentences and records ERPs as the subject reads the sentences. Which of the following sentences would you expect to show a characteristic response pattern on ERP recording?

   (a) The doctor was at the hospital
   (b) A dog chased the cat
   (c) Remembering is not forgotten
   (d) Flowers grow roots

(d) 3. An advantage of learning according to connectionist principles is that the network trains itself and can make inferences. Therefore it is said to successfully simulate human comprehension processes. Compared to human learning:

   (a) it parses at greater speeds
   (b) it can't create simple English sentences
   (c) its computational linguistics is more advanced
   (d) it is slower and requires more trials

(a) 4. The ATN uses a parsing strategy that "reads" syntactic states and transitions in a linear approach. Sometimes backtracking, reprocessing input in the light of new interpretations, is necessary because of information later in a sentence. Human parsing does not use this process, because

   (a) the capacity of working memory is too small
   (b) humans understand a reference when they encounter it the first time
   (c) we tend to write unambiguous sentences
   (d) only computers can reprocess input

(c) 5. A transition network represent the sentence *Mares eat oats* by the following format:

   (a) actor-action-object
   (b) subject-verb-object
   (c) a & b
   (d) none of the above

(b) 6. Joseph Weizenbaum attempted to simulate human understanding by a computer. He developed the program ELIZA, that

   (a) will someday replace psychiatrists
   (b) contained simple routines to rephrase and repeat input
   (c) was able to play chess with humans
   (d) could mimic language and parse sentences

(d) 7. The branch of cognitive psychology that investigates mental processes involved in language understanding and their relation to each other is

    (a) linguistics
    (b) neurolinguistics
    (c) syntactic analysis
    (d) psycholinguistics

(b) 8. Researchers who describe the structure of language apart from issues of comprehension are called

    (a) psycholinguists
    (b) linguists
    (c) psychologists
    (d) all of the above

(c) 9. A computer model designed to understand language based on a syntactic approach is known as

    (a) CTN
    (b) CAPS
    (c) ATN
    (d) all of the above

(d) 10. Researchers have grouped comprehension operations into three categories of processes. The processes used to generate a meaning representation from a sentence include

    (a) lexical, word-level, and syntactic processes
    (b) encoding, syntactic, and semantic processes
    (c) lexical access, grammatical and structural processes
    (d) lexical, syntactic, and semantic processes

(d) 11. Comprehension processes that operate independently are typically called

    (a) autonomous
    (b) interactive
    (c) contextual
    (d) modular

(a) 12. An index of comprehension that measures the duration of mental operations as they occur in time is known as an

    (a) on-line process
    (b) off-line process
    (c) real process
    (d) none of the above

(b) 13. The connectionist approach to comprehension proposes that the content of sentences and discourses is represented in

    (a) lists of propositions
    (b) distributed networks
    (c) semantic networks
    (d) a and b above

(b) 14. Theorists of the following approach propose that the content of sentences and discourses is represented in distributed networks

    (a) the symbolic processing approach
    (b) the connectionist approach
    (c) the propositional approach
    (d) none of the above

(c) 15. The process that transforms the physical word stimulus into a format that is compatible with the way the word's meaning is represented in the mental lexicon, is known as

    (a) recovery
    (b) comprehension
    (c) encoding
    (d) lexical access

(a) 16. Recovery of a word's meaning from long-term memory is known as

    (a) lexical access
    (b) encoding
    (c) comprehension
    (d) interpretation

(d) 17. The more characters a word has, the longer it takes to read. This is called the

    (a) frequency effect
    (b) encoding effect
    (c) context effect
    (d) none of the above

(a) 18. The frequency effect is a function of the following aspect of a word

    (a) familiarity
    (b) length
    (c) context
    (d) none of the above

(d) 19. The following hypothesis states that listeners attach incoming words to the most recently generated node

    (a) NVN strategy
    (b) content-word principle
    (c) end-a-constituent strategy
    (d) minimal attachment principle

(a) 20. According to the modular view of comprehension, encoding, lexical access, and syntactic process are characterized by the following relation

    (a) independence
    (b) interdependence
    (c) correlation
    (d) the relation depends on the semantic context

(d) 21. According to the serial encoding hypothesis, the encoding of words

    (a) is faster in a sentence context
    (b) is facilitated by characteristic shapes
    (c) is a function of their occurrence frequency in a language
    (d) none of the above

(b) 22. The result of the following operation is a transformation of a letter string into a form that can be read by the mental lexicon.

    (a) lexical access
    (b) encoding
    (c) comprehension
    (d) interpretation

(b) 23. The repository of information about words, including their spelling, meaning, relation to other words, and their syntactic role, is called

    (a) a grammar
    (b) the mental lexicon
    (c) syntax
    (d) all of the above

(c) 24. An author of the search theory of lexical access named in Chapter 11 is

    (a) Gough
    (b) Morton
    (c) Forster
    (d) McClelland

(c) 25. Direct-access models of lexical access tend to be

    (a) modular
    (b) contextual
    (c) interactive
    (d) more efficient

(a) 26. Search theorists believe entries in the lexicon are arranged

    (a) by the occurrence frequency of words
    (b) alphabetically
    (c) randomly
    (d) according to their semantic relations

(a) 27. According to the modular theory, lexical access

    (a) is independent of the sentence context
    (b) is dependent on the sentence context
    (c) interacts with the encoding process
    (d) involves a direct-access operation

(c) 28. The search theory of lexical access accounts for word context effects by assuming

    (a) a pre-access check
    (b) continuous checking
    (c) a post-access check
    (d) an interaction between sentence interpretation and lexical access

(c) 29. Interactive theorists believe context influences the recovery of a word's meaning _____ lexical access.

    (a) at the same time as
    (b) after
    (c) prior to
    (d) none of the above

(c) 30. In the following paradigm, a person receives acoustic and visual linguistic input.

    (a) bipolar receptor test
    (b) visual-phonological monitoring
    (c) bimodal lexical decision
    (d) dual input paradigm

(c) 31. The following model of lexical access holds that information from several levels of structure are continuously available for interpretation.

   (a) search theory
   (b) bimodal
   (c) direct-access
   (d) none of the above

(d) 32. Both interactive and modular theories of language processing can account for:

   (a) frequency effects
   (b) length effects
   (c) context effects
   (d) all of the above

(a) 33. Two connectionist researchers, St. John and McClelland, developed a parsing system based on connectionist principles. Their system

   (a) has no initial knowledge
   (b) has an initial set of syntactic categories
   (c) develops a set of rules as a result of training
   (d) mimics children's acquisition of verbs

(a) 34. Grouping words into phrases and segmenting sentences into clauses are examples of:

   (a) parsing
   (b) clausal grouping
   (c) chunking
   (d) forming propositions

(d) 35. According to the constituent strategy, listeners use the following to start a new constituent.

   (a) a noun
   (b) a content word
   (c) a conjunction
   (d) a function word

(c) 36. After listeners have identified the start of a constituent, they look for the following

   (a) a noun phrase
   (b) a noun
   (c) a content word
   (d) a function word

(b) 37. The following strategy was proposed to generate a meaning representation for simple SVO clauses of SVO languages.

    (a) Bever's
    (b) the Noun-verb-noun
    (c) the Find-a-constituent
    (d) the Begin-a-constituent

(d) 38. SVO languages account for how many of the world's languages?

    (a) about one half of all
    (b) nearly two thirds of all
    (c) nearly all
    (d) about one third of all

(d) 39. According to the Geschwind-Wernicke model on language processing

    (a) Geschwind's area is involved in comprehension, and Wernicke's area is responsible for production
    (b) Broca's area is responsible for production, and Wernicke's area is implicated in comprehension
    (c) language functions are distributed across the brain
    (d) none of the above

(a) 40. Electrical stimulation mapping research by Ojemann (1991) produced the following conclusions

    (a) language functions are localized in specific nuclei
    (b) language functions are localized in Broca's and Wernicke's areas
    (c) language production is localized while comprehension functions are distributed
    (d) language functions are distributed throughout the cortex

(d) 41. Patients suffering from Wernicke's aphasia exhibit the following symptom, among others

    (a) they have difficulty understanding function words
    (b) they have no apparent problems with production, but have significant comprehension problems
    (c) they tend to confuse function and content words
    (d) they have difficulty retrieving word meanings

(d) 42. According to psycholinguistic research, word stimuli are encoded by

    (a) being transferred to long-term memory
    (b) remaining in short-term memory
    (c) retrieving relevant information from long-term memory
    (d) transforming the word stimulus into a format that is compatible with the mental lexicon

(b) 43. According to Gernsbacher and Hargreaves' research, the following is used as the basis for the mental representation of a sentence.

    (a) deep structure of a sentence
    (b) foundational information
    (c) clausal boundaries
    (d) all of the above

(b) 44. According to research evidence presented in Chapter 11, readers use pauses at clause boundaries to

    (a) interpret the meaning of the prior clause
    (b) transfer information in the prior clause to a permanent representation
    (c) form a mental representation of the prior clause
    (d) transfer information in the prior clause to WM

(a) 45. The following reflects the semantic relations between the constituents of a sentence.

    (a) phrase marker
    (b) conjunction
    (c) interclausal pause
    (d) node of a phrase structure tree

(a) 46. The following acronym denotes a syntactic simulation model developed by computational linguists

    (a) ATN
    (b) CAPS
    (c) NVN
    (d) a & b above

(b) 47. The interpretation of discourse requires that the reader or listener must process the sentence in terms of

    (a) clauses
    (b) words
    (c) phrases
    (d) chunks

(b) 48. According to published accounts of the occurrence frequency of English words, which of the following is the most frequent word?

    (a) of
    (b) the
    (c) I
    (d) he

(a) 49. The effect of occurrence frequency on processing time is known as _____.

- (a) frequency effect
- (b) occurrence effect
- (c) length effect
- (d) context effect

(c) 50. The hypothesis is now widely accepted that words are encoded serially. Which of the following is not a reason to accept this hypothesis?

- (a) If reading is a visual analog of listening, as many believe, word encoding should be a serial process.
- (b) In speech, the phonemes of a word are created and transmitted serially; listeners receive phonemes serially.
- (c) In reading, people interpret the words one at a time from left to right.
- (d) In tachistoscopic recognition and lexical decision studies, word recognition times depend on word length.

(a) 51. Which model of word recognition postulates that the listener enters the string to be identified and searches entries stored in the lexicon until a match occurs between the string and an entry in the lexicon?

- (a) search models
- (b) direct-access models
- (c) template models
- (d) a and c only

(c) 52. Clear support for the _____ nature of lexical access comes from the bimodal lexical decision paradigm in which the person receives linguistic input from two modalities, acoustic and visual.

- (a) singular
- (b) interactive
- (c) modular
- (d) dynamic

(a) 53. _____ formulated six major syntactic strategies, including the Begin-A-Constituent strategy and Find-A-Content-Word strategy.

- (a) Clark and Clark
- (b) Aaronson and Scarborough
- (c) Just and Carpenter
- (d) St. John and McClelland

(c) 54. The following researcher(s) found that information from the initial clause is more accessible when it provides the foundation of the mental representation of the sentence.

- (a) Chan
- (b) Gernsbacher and Hargreaves
- (c) Aaronson and Scarborough
- (d) Martin

(c) 55. According to Gernsbacher and Hargreaves, information from _____ is more accessible when it provides the foundation of the mental representation of the sentence.

- (a) the most immediate clause
- (b) the middle clause
- (c) the first clause
- (d) none of the above

(b) 56. CAPS is a comprehensive system that involves parsing sentences and creating prepositions. The CAPS model

- (a) does not have a central executive
- (b) does have a central executive
- (c) is not empirically supported
- (d) B & C

(c) 57. _____ advance research on language understanding because they generate specific predictions which can be tested in experiments.

- (a) mental process models
- (b) direct access models
- (c) computational models
- (d) search models

(b) 58. Connectionist parsers differ from the ATN and CAPS models since

- (a) they have rules
- (b) they are not rule based
- (c) they are more reliable
- (d) they are more efficient

(b) 59. Which two variables influence a word's comprehension time?

- (a) word order and sentence structure
- (b) word length and word occurrence frequency
- (c) declarative sentence structure
- (d) speed of pronunciation

(c) 60. In word recognition studies, which words are most likely to be recognized more quickly?

    (a) polysyllabic words
    (b) infrequently used words
    (c) frequently used words
    (d) nouns

(a) 61. The context effect accords well with the hypothesis that holds that

    (a) initial information in a sentence to some extent predicts subsequent information
    (b) initial information is a poor predictor of subsequent information
    (c) subsequent information in a sentence is independent of initial information
    (d) understanding of content words depends on the word's environment

(d) 62. Barring exceptions, it is widely accepted that words are encoded:

    (a) in parallel
    (b) in groups
    (c) independently from
    (d) serially

(a) 63. In explaining the frequency effect, the direct access model assumes that:

    (a) a detector's activation threshold is lower for more frequent words
    (b) a detector's activation threshold is higher for more frequent words
    (c) a detector's activation threshold is lower for less frequent words
    (d) a detector's activation threshold is equal for frequent and infrequent words

(d) 64. Lexical access involves the recovery of the meaning of a word from the mental lexicon. Which of the following are two models of lexical access?

    (a) the Abstract theory and the Discrete theory
    (b) the Linguistic theory and the Logistic theory
    (c) the Comprehension theory and the Construction theory
    (d) the Direct Access theory and the Search theory

(b) 65. Comprehenders use strategies to group words into phrases, segment sentences into clauses, and generate a sentence structure. These strategies are called:

    (a) phrasing strategies
    (b) parsing strategies
    (c) causal strategies
    (d) retrieval strategies

(a) 66. The Modular Theory approach to language holds that:

   (a) different subprocesses of comprehension act independently, at least up to a point
   (b) information from several levels of structure are continuously available for interpretation
   (c) the frequency effect has no explanation
   (d) different parts of speech affect different modules of access

(a) 67. According to comprehension researcher, readers tend to segment sentences into clauses and exhibit brief reading pauses at clause boundaries. Presumably they do so in order to

   (a) transfer information from Working Memory to a more permanent representation
   (b) transfer information into Working Memory
   (c) resolve ambiguities in the previous clause
   (d) provide access to information in semantic memory

CHAPTER 12

(d) 1. It is easy to resume the story line when one is briefly interrupted during reading. According to Ericsson and Kintsch (1995), textual traces are quickly reinstated because they are held in

   (a) current passages
   (b) short-term working memory
   (c) a reading span
   (d) long-term working memory

(a) 2. There have been many theoretical models of dyslexia. Neuropsychological models link processing impairments with

   (a) abnormalities in specific brain areas
   (b) a pairing of visual and verbal symbols
   (c) alternate processing routes
   (d) limitations phonological processing

(c) 3. Neural networks may be trained to form associations between different types of symbols such as visual and verbal symbols. According to connectionist theorists, a disruption of such a network is believed to mimic

   (a) remedial reading programs
   (b) backward inferences
   (c) dyslexia
   (d) general illiteracy

(b) 4. Lateral masking refers to interference of a neighboring letter or word when the person identifies a target letter. Researchers found differences in the responses of normal and dyslexic readers to lateral masking. Specifically, they found that dyslexic readers are more confused by interference in their

    (a) right visual field
    (b) center visual field
    (c) previous text
    (d) verbal codes

(d) 5. In Chapter 12 several linguistic structures are named that are involved in reading comprehension. The following is not one of these.

    (a) letters
    (b) words
    (c) sentences
    (d) deep structures

(c) 6. The term "situation model" refers to the following

    (a) propositional model
    (b) text model
    (c) mental model
    (d) event model

(b) 7. Reading researchers express a text's ideas in terms of propositions. The proposition list is called

    (a) text memory
    (b) text base
    (c) deep structure
    (d) the foundation of the text

(b) 8. A proposition is

    (a) a list of arguments
    (b) a list of concepts
    (c) text representation
    (d) none of the above

(b) 9. When a noun appears for the first time in a text, it is known as a

    (a) an introductory noun
    (b) new argument noun
    (c) repeated argument
    (d) unique noun

(b) 10. Select the proposition from among the following items

    (a) (JOHN, READ, BOOK)
    (b) (INTERESTING, BOOK)
    (c) (HOUSE, YELLOW)
    (d) (MARY, SLEEPS)

(c) 11. According to Kintsch's notation, a proposition includes the following order of concepts

    (a) (verb, noun,...)
    (b) (noun phrase, verb phrase,...)
    (c) (predicate, argument,...)
    (d) (subject, predicate,...)

(d) 12. The concept "blue" in the proposition (BLUE, BALL) expresses the

    (a) adjective
    (b) subject
    (c) argument
    (d) none of the above

(a) 13. The coherence of a passage of text is expressed by the following

    (a) repeated arguments
    (b) list of propositions
    (c) foundational concepts
    (d) new argument nouns

(c) 14. The process whereby a reader links information from the text with text memory is called

    (a) memory access
    (b) laying a foundation
    (c) integration
    (d) argument cycling

(a) 15. Because of the limitations of working memory, Kintsch and van Dijk (1978) have postulated that the reader interprets a text

    (a) in sequential cycles
    (b) in long-term memory
    (c) in parallel
    (d) one proposition at a time

(b) 16. The concept that a repeated argument refers to is known as a(n)

   (a) anaphoric reference
   (b) antecedent
   (c) new argument
   (d) propositional concept

(a) 17. A reference to an earlier concept of a repeated argument is known as an

   (a) anaphoric reference
   (b) antecedent reference
   (c) new argument reference
   (d) propositional reference

(b) 18. The same-gender strategy is a strategy that helps identify

   (a) anaphoric references
   (b) antecedents
   (c) new arguments
   (d) pronominal precedents

(a) 19. In computer based word-for-word reading experiments, reading times typically do the following at the boundary of a clause or sentence

   (a) increase
   (b) decrease
   (c) remain unchanged
   (d) increase or decrease depending upon the complexity of the clause or sentence.

(c) 20. When sentences are not immediately coherent readers make the following types of inferences

   (a) elaborative inferences
   (b) forward inferences
   (c) bridging inferences
   (d) all of the above

(c) 21. Consider the following sentence pair: "Mary put the lunch on the table. The bread was still crisp." Readers are said to link these sentences via a/an

   (a) elaborative inference
   (b) forward inference
   (c) bridging inference
   (d) none of the above

(a) 22. The following researchers investigated bridging inferences in reading

   (a) Haviland & Clark
   (b) Kintsch & van Dijk
   (c) Just & Carpenter
   (d) Gernsbacher & Hargreaves

(d) 23. The following researchers demonstrated that readers do not draw forward inferences during comprehension

   (a) Haviland & Clark
   (b) St. John & McClelland
   (c) Just & Carpenter
   (d) McKoon & Ratcliff

(d) 24. According to Kintsch and van Dijk, readers transfer propositions via x to y.

   (a) x: the carry-over buffer; y: text memory
   (b) x: text memory; y: working memory
   (c) x: text memory; y: the carry-over buffer
   (d) x: working memory; y: text memory

(b) 25. Researchers have found that sentences with more causal links to prior sentences

   (a) took longer to read because the reader had to integrate more information
   (b) were better recalled because information was better integrated
   (c) were poorly recalled because there was more interference among the many links
   (d) were read more quickly because the information was more readily integrated

(b) 26. Crowder (1982) observed the reading patterns of a dyslexic woman. Like other dyslexic individuals, this woman

   (a) had great difficulty in reading the passage aloud
   (b) encountered no difficulties in reading the passage aloud
   (c) remembered the information in the passage surprisingly well
   (d) could not distinguish between old and new information in sentences

(c) 27. A person is diagnosed as dyslexic when she or he

   (a) has general reading difficulties
   (b) has a reading level not compatible with his or her IQ
   (c) has a lower reading level than predicted by his or her IQ
   (d) can read texts aloud but not comprehend their content

(d) 28. Speed reading programs

    (a) are effective because they encourage better concentration
    (b) are effective because they teach students to gain control over their eye fixations
    (c) are ineffective because they fail to improve peripheral vision and previewing
    (d) none of the above

(b) 29. The most effective way of increasing one's reading speed, according to reading researchers is the following

    (a) take a speed reading course
    (b) do background reading on the material you wish to read
    (c) train yourself to concentrate better and attend to central ideas of the passage
    (d) increase your effective vocabulary and thus speed up the lexical-access component of reading

(d) 30. Cognitive psychologists identify two reasons for the alleged decline in literacy. These include:

    (a) increased TV viewing
    (b) less time spent reading
    (c) usage of simple language construction in TV programs
    (d) a and b above

(d) 31. Researchers of writing composition have adopted a componential framework of writing. According to this framework, the principal components of composition are:

    (a) the writer and the text
    (b) the text and the environment
    (c) the writer and the audience
    (d) a and b above

(b) 32. Writing composition is said to involve the following four stages. Choose the stage during which propositions are entered into working memory, according to composition researchers.

    (a) planning
    (b) making meaning
    (c) expressing meaning
    (d) reviewing

(c) 33. Composition teachers have recommended techniques for generating ideas for a paper. One such technique involves

    (a) reviewing paper
    (b) expressing meaning
    (c) considering contrasts
    (d) making meaning

(c) 34. Transforming is best described by a declarative memory representation into an external representation on a page or screen.

- (a) planning
- (b) making meaning
- (c) expressing meaning
- (d) reviewing

(a) 35. The following is a linear sequence of words that conforms to the syntactic rules of language.

- (a) sentence
- (b) clause
- (c) proposition
- (d) concept

(d) 36. The author's evaluation of meaning relative to an audience is best described as

- (a) planning
- (b) making meaning
- (c) expressing meaning
- (d) reviewing

(c) 37. The sentence "Mike hit the ball" implies that Mike used a bat to hit the ball. Suppose a listener were to infer that implication. Such an inference is known as

- (a) backward
- (b) bridging
- (c) forward
- (d) argumentative

(d) 38. According to the Kintsch and Dijk model, readers transfer propositions from ____ to ____.

- (a) working memory to the text base
- (b) working memory to long term memory
- (c) text memory to short term memory
- (d) none of the above

(b) 39. Links between adjacent propositions are maintained through one or more propositions stored in a

- (a) text base
- (b) carry-over buffer
- (c) text memory
- (d) carry-over sentence

(b) 40. Dyslexia can be described by all of the following except:

   (a) a person reads at a level below the expected level
   (b) a person has a problem naming the letters of the target word
   (c) a person can read aloud but not comprehend what they say
   (d) a person has difficulty identifying target words

(a) 41. How many new arguments are there in the following passage: "The Greeks loved beautiful art. When the Romans conquered the Greeks, they copied them, and thus learned to create beautiful art."

   (a) 3
   (b) 5
   (c) 10
   (d) 21

(b) 42. According to Robinson's SQR3 approach, which involves establishing links between new and familiar information?

   (a) integration
   (b) deep processing
   (c) decoding
   (d) reviewing

(c) 43. According to Robinson's method of reading comprehension, all of the following steps can be included to improve one's memory for information in a text except:

   (a) surveying
   (b) reciting
   (c) scanning
   (d) reading

(a) 44. In terms of Kintsch and van Dijk's model, the reader links information from the text with text memory. This process is known as

   (a) integration
   (b) deep processing
   (c) decoding
   (d) reviewing

(c) 45. A good definition of *text memory* is:

   (a) inferences taken from the text and chunked in memory
   (b) elaborations based on the text and integrated with memory
   (c) the text's ideas represented as propositions in memory
   (d) a simplified model of the reader's full knowledge of the text

(c) 46. The *text base* is formed by:

   (a) inferences taken from the text
   (b) elaborations made from the text
   (c) a list of propositions based on the text
   (d) a simplified model of the reader's full knowledge of the text

(a) 47. Reading times tend to increase immediately when:

   (a) a reader encounters a new argument noun
   (b) a reader finishes reading a phrase
   (c) a reader encounters a repeated argument noun
   (d) a reader encounters a question

(c) 48. Due to the limited capacity of working memory:

   (a) much information from a given text is not stored
   (b) details are considered extraneous and therefore not stored
   (c) input is processed in cycles
   (d) input must be processed in parallel

(d) 49. One difference between normal readers and dyslexic readers is that 96% of

   (a) dyslexic patients have comprehension difficulties whether they listen or read
   (b) normal readers exhibit a greater number of regressive eye movements
   (c) normal readers fixate longer on words
   (d) none of the above

(b) 50. The best way to increase reading speed while maintaining comprehension is:

   (a) to zig zag scan across the page
   (b) to become familiar with the content of the passage
   (c) to use more peripheral vision
   (d) make more inferences

(c) 51. The four major components of the writing process are

   (a) argument, counterargument, reiteration, resolution
   (b) discretion, evaluation, enumeration, explanation
   (c) planning, making meaning, expressing meaning, reviewing the text
   (d) author, environment, audience, meaning

(b) 52. The four component processes of writing

   (a) are discrete, no overlap occurs
   (b) overlap, frequently occurring simultaneously
   (c) can happen in any order

(d) are not universal

(c) 53. According to Kellogg, using an outline

(a) improves the efficiency of writing
(b) stifles creativity
(c) improves the quality of the text
(d) has no effect on the final paper

(b) 54. According to Chapter 12, which of the following best defines the act of reading?

(a) empathizing with the protagonist of a story
(b) selecting ideas from the printed page
(c) making inferences from the text
(d) understanding the cognitive processes involved in analyzing a text

(a) 55. Which of the following captures the major content of the passage and its spatial and temporal relations?

(a) mental model
(b) text memory
(c) text base
(d) new argument noun

(b) 56. According to Chapter 12, which of the following terms refers to the process by which a reader links the information from a text with her text memory?

(a) selection
(b) integration
(c) transfer
(d) proposition

(c) 57. According to Chapter 12, which of the following terms best represents reference to an antecedent?

(a) argument noun
(b) anaphoric reference
(c) bridging inference
(d) none of the above

(d) 58. According to McKoon and Ratcliff's (1986) study, which of the following inference(s) do readers not make when trying to comprehend a text?

(a) bridging inference
(b) backward inference
(c) forward inference
(d) causal inference

(d) 59. Which of the following best describes what a function word does?

- (a) it conveys the meaning of a sentence
- (b) it describes the function of constituents
- (c) it helps a writer to organize sentence production
- (d) it signals the syntactic structure of a sentence

(a) 60. Which of the following are the five steps of Robinson's SQR3 method for improving memory of the textual material?

- (a) survey, questions, read, recite, review
- (b) study, questions, read, recite, review
- (c) study, questions, read, review, reintegrate
- (d) survey, questions, recite, reintegrate, review

CHAPTER 13

(c) 1. Differences in mathematical ability as a function of gender are small. Exposure and contexts play an important role in testing performance. While males do better on quantitative SAT scores

- (a) cognitive abilities are unimportant
- (b) it may be due to less interest among female test takers
- (c) differences are greater within a gender than between enders
- (d) this occurs because they are not willing to guess on answers

(b) 2. According to Reber (1993), transfer of problem solving occurs when

- (a) LOGO learning is involved
- (b) structurally similarity and shared rules occur
- (c) people don't over generalize
- (d) a balance-scale problem is used

(d) 3. "Functional fixedness" is a phrase used by Gestalt psychologists. It describes limits in problem solving and general intelligence

- (a) caused by over coaching and cramming
- (b) due to improper encoding
- (c) caused by changing definitions
- (d) due to an inability to consider alternatives

(c) 4. Metacognitive ability, observing your own problem solving efforts, is useful for evaluating solutions. This is usually considered a skill of intelligent individuals.

- (a) It is an example of limited generalization
- (b) Early neural development is involved
- (c) This ability can improve with training and development
- (d) Einstein used this as the base of his Relativity theory

(b) 5. Problems whose solutions are largely based on general problem solving strategies are called

   (a) knowledge-rich problems
   (b) knowledge-lean problems
   (c) well-defined problems
   (d) ill-defined problems

(a) 6. Problems whose solutions require much specialized knowledge in a particular domain are called

   (a) knowledge-rich problems
   (b) knowledge-lean problems
   (c) well-defined problems
   (d) ill-defined problems

(b) 7. Problems in which letters represent digits are called

   (a) word arithmetic problems
   (b) cryptarithmetic
   (c) geometric analogy
   (d) story analogy

(b) 8. The following types of problems have clearly defined initial and goal states and operators available to permit transition between states

   (a) specific
   (b) well-defined
   (c) knowledge-rich
   (d) knowledge-lean

(a) 9. In the following types of problems, the goal state must be inferred

   (a) ill-defined
   (b) well-defined
   (c) knowledge-rich
   (d) knowledge-lean

(c) 10. An action which moves the problem solver from one state in the problem space to another is called

   (a) solution path
   (b) subgoal
   (c) operator
   (d) strategy

(d) 11. Which of the following is an example of a well-defined problem?

(a) choosing a job
(b) composing a term paper
(c) diagnosing a disease
(d) an algebra problem

(a) 12. Which of the following is an example of an ill-defined problem?

(a) finding the cause of car trouble
(b) a geometry problem
(c) a computer programming task
(d) a game

(b) 13. The description of the problem's universe at a particular point in time is known as

(a) solution path
(b) state
(c) schema
(d) representation

(a) 14. Any sequence of operators that connect the initial and goal states of a problem is called the

(a) solution path
(b) problem search
(c) problem schema
(d) heuristic search

(b) 15. When a problem solver uses rules of thumb to cut down the search space and find a solution path to a problem, she is using

(a) search
(b) heuristic search
(c) means-ends strategy
(d) insight

(d) 16. The type of problem solving that involves asking two questions: 1) What is the biggest difference between the initial and goal states? and 2) How can this difference be reduced?

(a) pyramid subgoal strategy
(b) analogy strategy
(c) general problem-solving strategy
(d) none of the above

(a) 17. When an operator is blocked by some obstacle, the problem solver removes the obstacle by

    (a) setting a subgoal
    (b) engaging in a heuristic search
    (c) using meta-cognition
    (d) reducing the difference between the current state and the goal state

(b) 18. A strategy that repeatedly calls upon itself until a problem is solved is known as a

    (a) subgoal strategy
    (b) recursive strategy
    (c) meta-cognitive strategy
    (d) general problem-solving strategy

(a) 19. Newell and Simon's General Problem Solver is based on

    (a) the means-end strategy
    (b) a computer simulation
    (c) the Tower of Hanoi problem
    (d) a & c

(c) 20. The General Problem Solver was developed by the following researchers

    (a) Russell and Whitehead
    (b) Anzai and Simon
    (c) Simon and Newell
    (d) Kotovsky and Simon

(d) 21. In the Tower of Hanoi Problem, the problem solver tries to move a pyramid of disks one at a time, from peg 1 to 3. Let's assume there are three disks, A, B, and C, and the person is just starting out. Also assume that A is the smallest disk, and C the largest one. Remember that certain constraints apply. Optimally, the first two moves would be the following

    (a) 1: C to 3, 2: B to 3
    (b) 1: A to 3, 2: B to 3
    (c) 1: A to 2, 2: B to 3
    (d) 1: A to 3, 2: B to 2

(d) 22. The Tower of Hanoi Problem involves the movement of x disks over y pegs

    (a) x: any number, y: any number
    (b) x: any number, y: four pegs
    (c) x: four disks, y: three pegs
    (d) x: any number, y: three pegs

(a) 23. The advantage of the following strategy of solving the Tower of Hanoi problem is that it separates mental plans from physical moves

    (a) pyramid subgoal strategy
    (b) means-ends strategy
    (c) general problem-solving strategy
    (d) disk-and-peg strategy

(a) 24. The subgoal strategy is difficult because the problem solver must

    (a) generate the sequence of subgoals and remember them
    (b) remember the goal, the number of disks, and their position
    (c) execute the subgoals in a sequential order
    (d) execute the subgoals in parallel

(b) 25. The following problem type involves objects of different sizes being moved between physical locations

    (a) change
    (b) transfer
    (c) analogous
    (d) isomorphic

(a) 26. The following problem type involves altering the properties of objects

    (a) change
    (b) transfer
    (c) analogous
    (d) isomorphic

(c) 27. Production systems provide a notation to represent procedural knowledge. They have been used to capture processes that underlie problem solving. Production systems

    (a) represent information in a distributed network
    (b) are a useful notation for problem solving but not capable of learning
    (c) simulate subjects' problem solving performance
    (d) none of the above

(c) 28. Problems with a common structure are analogous. Researchers have found that subjects

    (a) typically use the similarity between analogous problems to their advantage
    (b) discover the similarity between analogous problems, but their solution time is not changed
    (c) typically do not discover the similarity of analogous problems
    (d) usually solve analogy problems by insight

(d) 29. According to Holyoak and Thagard (1989) analogy problems are solved by

   (a) applying a set of production rules in sequence
   (b) using a recursive subgoal strategy
   (c) discovering the common knowledge base of the two problems
   (d) satisfying multiple constraints in parallel

(b) 30. In the Tower of Hanoi puzzle, a disk move represents the following

   (a) a subgoal
   (b) an operator
   (c) a state
   (d) a final goal

(b) 31. The difficulty in the means-end strategy lies in the fact that there are too many subgoals. The way to overcome this is the use of:

   (a) substrategies
   (b) external memory aids
   (c) mnemonics
   (d) internal memory aids

(c) 32. The following is a representation of arithmetic facts in long term memory that accounts for problem solvers' error patterns

   (a) Table Search Model
   (b) Network Retrieval Model
   (c) Distribution of Associations Hypothesis
   (d) Means-End Strategy

(c) 33. Heuristic search strategies:

   (a) lengthen search time but increase accuracy
   (b) always work
   (c) work frequently
   (d) are based on extensive knowledge of the problem domain

(b) 34. The means-end strategy is

   (a) a recursive strategy that focuses on the overall goal
   (b) a recursive strategy in which the problem solver adopts sub-goals
   (c) a strategy that seeks to achieve the goal in terms of plans
   (d) a recursive strategy that fails if an obstacle is encountered

(d) 35. The following is a difficulty with the means-end strategy:

   (a) it is not a general strategy
   (b) it is not applicable to ill-defined problems
   (c) it is too time-consuming
   (d) too many subgoals tax working memory

(c) 36. Although Einstein was a genius in physics, he reportedly was unable to balance his checkbook. One explanation for this is that:

   (a) Einstein was frequently absent minded
   (b) people are just naturally smart in certain domains
   (c) a person is usually an expert in only one domain
   (d) none of the above

(c) 37. Observing one's own problem-solving activity is a(n)

   (a) introspective activity
   (b) recursive activity
   (c) meta-cognitive activity
   (d) domain-specific activity

(a) 38. According to cognitive psychologists, one principal source of difference between individuals that are considered intelligent and individuals that are not is:

   (a) intelligent individuals tend to allocate working memory resources better
   (b) intelligent individuals are highly self-aware and better able to monitor their responses
   (c) the difference is only apparent; people who do less well on tests are often more successful in real life
   (d) less intelligent individuals cannot distinguish important information from irrelevant detail

(d) 39. Kaplan and Simon emphasize the importance of choosing an appropriate representation as an essential part of problem solving. In the example of searching for a diamond in a long, dark hall, the subject first searches the floor inch by inch, but after more thought she looks for a lightswitch instead. Once the light is on, the diamond can be more easily found. This is what Kaplan and Simon consider to be:

   (a) searching within a representation
   (b) searching without a representation
   (c) searching through a representation
   (d) searching for a representation

(b) 40. Gestalt psychologists describe an individual's inability to consider alternative perspectives as:

   (a) ambiguous input
   (b) functional fixedness
   (c) incorrect encoding
   (d) schema-based problem solving

(b) 41. Investigators have found that coaching

   (a) results in substantial gains in score on aptitude tests
   (b) does help performance on achievement tests
   (c) gains are attributable to cognitive rather that motivational factors
   (d) can achieve much the same effect as long term education

(c) 42. Solving a problem through search requires finding a path that leads from the starting state to the goal state. This is known as

   (a) subgoal strategy
   (b) an heuristic
   (c) a solution path
   (d) none of the above

(d) 43. Expert knowledge is _____ and _____.

   (a) general and transfers to other domains
   (b) specific and transfers to other domains
   (c) general and does not transfer to other domains
   (d) specific and does not transfer to other domains

(b) 44. An expert's understanding of knowledge is

   (a) inferred
   (b) procedural
   (c) deliberate
   (d) none of the above

(c) 45. In young children, mathematical operations are

   (a) covert
   (b) learned
   (c) overt
   (d) schema based

(d) 46. The Tower of Hanoi problem is an example of which of the following problem types?

   (a) knowledge-rich
   (b) operator
   (c) meta-cognitive
   (d) knowledge-lean

(b) 47. Which of the following is an action that moves a problem from one state to another?

   (a) procedure
   (b) operator
   (c) solution path
   (d) protocol

(a) 48. Which of the following definitions best describes the subgoal strategy?

   (a) if the operator is blocked by an obstacle, the problem solver removes the obstacle before continuing
   (b) the problem solver cuts down search space by using rules of thumb
   (c) the problem solver talks aloud while he is solving the problem
   (d) the problem solver must reduce the difference between the initial problem state and the goal state by using operators

(c) 49. One of the reasons why the monster change problem is more difficult than the Tower of Hanoi problem is the following:

   (a) the Tower of Hanoi problem has isomorphs whereas the monster change problem does not
   (b) people have more trouble using monsters and spheres rather than pegs and rings
   (c) people have more practice transferring objects between locations than varying their sizes
   (d) none of the reasons given above are valid

(b) 50. Several production systems have been introduced to mimic human problem solving. Which of the following best describes PRISM?

   (a) it simulates a wide range of cognitive actions and represents them in terms of the problem solving model of transforming states from an initial state to a goal state
   (b) it learns and modifies its production as a result of experience
   (c) it is a general cognitive architecture that includes problem solving skills and other cognitive skills which mimic human thinking
   (d) it is a connectionist model using principles of constraint satisfaction as in pattern recognition to simulate problem solving in a variety of situations

(d) 51. Which of the following is not a distinctive feature between experts and novices?

(a) expert knowledge is procedural and novice knowledge is not
(b) experts understand problems more deeply than do novices
(c) experts can evaluate their solution paths whereas novices stay fixated on one particular path
(d) experts usually exhibit greater memory capacity than novices

(a) 52. Which of the following models of mathematical representations proposed by Siegler has two sets of nodes for the operands, one set for the results, and includes an explanation of how an error was committed?

(a) the distribution of associations hypothesis
(b) the network retrieval method
(c) the analogical constraint mapping engine
(d) the table search model

(d) 53. Which of the following is true of the transfer of training view, according to chapter 13?

(a) it facilitates general problem solving skills for any type of problems
(b) it helps problem solvers in solving analogy problems
(c) it facilitates a student's learning of languages and other cognitive skills
(d) it facilitates the solving of problems that contain similar components

(a) 54. According to Siegler (1991), a child's ability to find a solution to a problem improves with age. Which of the following does Siegler attribute this development to?

(a) improvements in memory and content knowledge
(b) development of information processing skills
(c) increase in the child's motivation to solve a problem
(d) gain in cognitive resources and ability to classify a problem

(c) 55. In the mutilated chessboard puzzle, which of the following facilitates solution of the problem?

(a) thinking of the chessboard as a rectangle, not a square
(b) thinking of dominoes and chess as games, not problems
(c) representing the chessboard in terms of the color of squares
(d) thinking at first of the chessboard without the two columns of squares on either side

(b) 56. According to Kulik et al. (1984), which of the following is not true about SAT coaching sessions?

(a) they yield motivational rather than cognitive gains
(b) they reduce the student's test anxiety and help her to obtain a higher score
(c) they increase SAT scores by about 30 points on average
(d) they cause the learner to invest much time and effort into solving the problems

(d) 57. Which of the following factors contribute, according to cognitive psychologists, to differences in intelligence?

    (a) encoding speed, retrieval speed, and academic achievement
    (b) encoding speed, allocation of working memory resources, and new perspectives on problems
    (c) being "street-smart," encoding speed, and long-term memory
    (d) allocation of working memory resources, encoding speed, and retrieval speed

(c) 58. What is the principal difference between Siegler's 1988 Network Retrieval Model and the Distribution of Associations hypothesis?

    (a) the network retrieval model is used for multiplication and division, and the distribution of associations hypothesis is used for addition and subtraction
    (b) the distribution of associations hypothesis creates two links between operands and results whereas the network retrieval model creates only one
    (c) the distribution of associations hypothesis includes an explanation of how the problem solver commits errors while the network retrieval model does not
    (d) the network retrieval model's links between nodes are direct while the distribution of associations hypothesis has more links for larger operations

CHAPTER 14

(b) 1. Rules of proof, such as *Modus Pones* and *Modus Tollens*, arrive at a conclusion by strict adherence to formal logic. This form of logic is referred to as

    (a) generalized to fit set of observations
    (b) deductive reasonin
    (c) inductive reasoning
    (d) based on hypothesis consistency

(d) 2. If you ask people they will tell you they like having choices. However, research shows that we react differently according to available alternatives.

    (a) People prefer a wide range of choices
    (b) More choice lowers conflict of decision
    (c) Alternatives aid our decision process in all conditions
    (d) Choices are influenced by the number of alternatives

(c) 3. Cognitive psychologists have found that people reason based on content and context. Unlike the normative aspects of reasoning that logicians emphasize, psychologists study

    (a) how people should reason
    (b) what neurochemicals are involved
    (c) how people do reason
    (d) like the size of the task involved

(a) 4. According to the Rescorla-Wagner (1972) rule, assessing cues on relative validity rather than absolute validity, determines

    (a) its associative effectiveness
    (b) fewer conditioned responses
    (c) the extent to which we correlate the probability
    (d) its true purpose

(b) 5. In inductive reasoning tasks the subject attempts

    (a) to verify a specific hypothesis based on general principles
    (b) to discover a generalization that fits a set of observations
    (c) to verify a conclusion given a set of premises
    (d) to discover the principle that underlies a pattern of letters or numbers

(c) 6. The rule that fits the following sequence of numbers "52, 23, 70, 51, 27, 65, 50, 31, 60, ..." is based on

    (a) a cycle of single numbers
    (b) a cycle of pairs of numbers
    (c) a cycle of three numbers
    (d) a cycle of four numbers

(b) 7. A concept is

    (a) an abstract principle used by perceivers to categorize events in time and space
    (b) the representation of a set of attributes shared by members of a class
    (c) a representation of the typical features of the members of a category
    (d) none of the above

(c) 8. The following notion postulates that learners generate hunches to express the relation between stimuli and labels.

    (a) equilibrium theory
    (b) prototype-evaluation theory
    (c) hypothesis-testing theory
    (d) stimulus-discrimination theory

(d) 9. A subject in a concept formation task who changes her current hypothesis when told that she is wrong uses the

    (a) subtraction strategy
    (b) elimination strategy
    (c) no-memory strategy
    (d) none of the above

(c) 10. The following entity allows organisms to infer properties from a perceptual pattern

   (a) hypothesis
   (b) induction
   (c) category
   (d) decision tree

(d) 11. The process subjects use to group instances in terms of their similarity and variability is called

   (a) series completion
   (b) probabilistic reasoning
   (c) hypothesis testing
   (d) categorization

(b) 12. A posterior probability refers to the probability that

   (a) a property exists in the population given a certain trait
   (b) a hypothesis is true given certain evidence
   (c) evidence is significant given a specific trait
   (d) a patient has a disease given a certain symptom

(d) 13. In medicine, a conditional probability refers to

   (a) a symptom's probability in the population given a certain criterion
   (b) the probability of a diagnosis given a specific symptom
   (c) the probability of a disease given a set of symptoms
   (d) the probability of a symptom given the disease

(d) 14. Bayes' theorem is used to calculate

   (a) a prior probability
   (b) a base-rate probability
   (c) a conditional probability
   (d) a posterior probability

(c) 15. Gluck and Bower (1988) investigated probabilistic category learning in a quasi medical setting. Subjects were told that a group of patients exhibited one of two diseases. They were also given a set of symptoms associated with each of the diseases. Next subjects were given over 200 charts of patients' symptoms; they were asked to diagnose the disease and then the subjects were give feedback. The researchers found that subjects

   (a) were not able to diagnose the patients' disease
   (b) learned to give the proper weight to each of symptoms
   (c) were unduly influenced by representative symptoms
   (d) underestimated the base-rate of the diseases

(d) 16. In simulated medical diagnosis problems, subjects associate a property with a concept more strongly after undergoing

    (a) connectionist training
    (b) Bayesian training
    (c) conditional training
    (d) contingent training

(a) 17. Subjects tend to select an attribute as most predictive of a reinforcement even though the number of pairings of each attribute and the concept was equal. This reflects

    (a) the selective learning effect
    (b) base-rate neglect
    (c) the representative heuristic
    (d) the conjunction fallacy

(b) 18. Consider premises (1) and (2), then indicate the correct conclusion. (1) If Mary is busy, then the lawn will be blue. (2) The lawn is not blue.

    (a) Therefore Mary is busy
    (b) Therefore Mary is not busy
    (c) Therefore the lawn is green
    (d) none of the above

(c) 19. Wason and Johnson-Laird developed the selection task. In this task, subjects were shown four cards that have a letter on one side and a number on the other. They were also given a conditional statement and were asked to test the truth of the statement by selecting specific evidence that would either confirm or disconfirm it. Assume subjects saw the following cards
                         A   D   4   7
and the statement "If a card has a vowel on one side, then it has an even number on the other side." Which of the cards must be turned over to determine if this statement is valid or not?

    (a) A and 4
    (b) D and 7
    (c) A and 7
    (d) D and 4

(b) 20. When one discovers a hypothesis consistent with a body of data or experience, one practices reasoning of the following type

    (a) deductive
    (b) inductive
    (c) probabilisitic
    (d) all of the above

(d) 21. Assume subjects are given a list of items and asked to form a rule that predicts subsequent items. This type of task is known as

    (a) concept learning
    (b) hypothesis-testing
    (c) blank-trial
    (d) series completion

(a) 22. In the following research paradigm, experimenters present a set of items with different attributes, one of which defines a category or concept.

    (a) concept learning
    (b) hypothesis-testing
    (c) blank-trial
    (d) series completion

(d) 23. According to Gestalt psychology creativity involves

    (a) finding new ways of doing something
    (b) going beyond the information given
    (c) breaking the bounds of entrenched habits and beliefs
    (d) restructuring of stimulus cues

(c) 24. One of the first researchers who sought to investigate creativity empirically was Sir Francis Galton. After much research, Galton concluded that

    (a) creativity was too elusive for empirical study after all
    (b) creativity was the result of painstaking preparation
    (c) creativity was inherited
    (d) creativity was based on insight

(b) 25. The computer program that uses a production system to discover regularities in a set of data and rediscovered Kepler's law

    (a) KEPLER
    (b) BACON
    (c) SIMON
    (d) ACT

(a) 26. According to such researchers as Gardner, the following quality is usually found among creative geniuses

    (a) tolerance for uncertainty
    (b) an extraordinary memory capacity
    (c) ability to produce episodes of insight
    (d) ability to imagine new stimulus arrangements

(a) 27. The following is a type of fallacy committed when one judges an event more likely because of its similarity to a prototype

       (a) the representativeness heuristic
       (b) the conjunction fallacy
       (c) the gambler's fallacy
       (d) the prototype bias

(b) 28. According to the following statement, the probability of two events occurring cannot exceed the probability of one of those events

       (a) representativeness heuristic
       (b) conjunction rule
       (c) availability heuristic
       (d) base-rate rule

(d) 29. When a person erroneously believes an event of two joint properties is more likely to occur than each property by itself, he commits

       (a) base-rate neglect
       (b) the gambler's fallacy
       (c) the availability fallacy
       (d) the conjunction fallacy

(d) 30. A subject tends to underestimate the occurrence of long runs of similar events due to

       (a) the conjunction fallacy
       (b) base-rate neglect
       (c) the availability fallacy
       (d) the gambler's <u>fallacy</u>

(c) 31. When we overestimate the probability of an event's occurrence because we perceive or remember it well, we commit

       (a) the conjunction fallacy
       (b) the gambler's fallacy
       (c) the availability fallacy
       (d) base-rate neglect

(c) 32. Utility is a concept used by economists and psychologists alike. According to cognition researchers, utility

       (a) measures the quantitative gain a person achieves in problem solving
       (b) measures the subjective gain a person achieves in problem solving
       (c) is an indication of how well an outcome satisfies a goal
       (d) none of the above

(a) 33. If a decision maker favors choice A over B, and choice B over C, then he will favor choice A over choice C. This illustrates the

   (a) transitivity principle
   (b) dominance principle
   (c) invariance principle
   (d) compatibility principle

(b) 34. If one choice is favored on the basis of one attribute, and is considered at least equal on all other attributes, it will be chosen. This is an example of the

   (a) transitivity principle
   (b) dominance principle
   (c) invariance principle
   (d) compatibility principle

(c) 35. The following principle says that if the same underlying choice is presented in different contexts, it will produce the same preference.

   (a) transitivity principle
   (b) dominance principle
   (c) invariance principle
   (d) compatibility principle

(a) 36. The act of choosing an alternative that meets a current goal while avoiding negative consequences

   (a) maximizes utilities
   (b) satisfies a goal
   (c) reflects the win-stay, lose-shift strategy
   (d) reflects selective learning

(b) 37. Decision makers are influenced by the context used in stating alternatives. This is referred to as

   (a) the invariance principle
   (b) the framing effect
   (c) holistic processing
   (d) none of the above

(a) 38. Tversky and Kahneman conducted important research on choice behavior and risk taking. According to their research, people tend

   (a) to perceive choice alternatives, but they avoid risks
   (b) not to perceive all choice alternatives but are willing to take risks
   (c) to take risks in choices involving gain and avoid risks in choices involving loss
   (d) to take risks in choices involving loss and avoid risks in choices involving gain

(b) 39. The process whereby a decision maker considers one aspect of a choice across alternatives is called

- (a) holistic processing
- (b) dimensional processing
- (c) lexicographic processing
- (d) the elimination-by-aspects strategy

(a) 40. The process whereby a decision maker considers all dimensions of each alternative is called

- (a) holistic processing
- (b) dimensional processing
- (c) lexicographic processing
- (d) the global focussing strategy

(b) 41. According to the following decision making strategy, one combines measures of attributes to give an overall quality score for each choice.

- (a) lexicographic
- (b) additive
- (c) elimination-by-aspects
- (d) global focussing

(a) 42. In the following decision making strategy, the most important attribute of a problem is emphasized and all others ignored.

- (a) lexicographic
- (b) additive
- (c) elimination-by-aspects
- (d) global focussing

(b) 43. A graphic representation that captures diverse choice situations.

- (a) flow chart
- (b) decision tree
- (c) value function
- (d) all of the above

(d) 44. When decision makers weigh more heavily attributes that are most compatible with the type of response required, they use the following decision making principle

- (a) transitivity principle
- (b) dominance principle
- (c) invariance principle
- (d) compatibility principle

(a) 45. According to the following notion, organisms seek a bliss point and allocate time to activities in order to maintain the status quo.

   (a) equilibrium theory
   (b) the representative heuristic
   (c) hypothesis-testing theory
   (d) the compatibility principle

(d) 46. Students as well as the BACON simulation used discovery heuristics and rediscovered principles first proposed by

   (a) Kekulé
   (b) Simon
   (c) Einstein
   (d) Kepler

(b) 47. The following heuristic compares events to a prototype, and selects the more likely event.

   (a) Discovery
   (b) Representativeness
   (c) Availability
   (d) Probabilistic

(c) 48. Underestimating the likelihood of long runs refers to which of the following?

   (a) Conjunction Fallacy
   (b) Probabilistic Fallacy
   (c) Gambler's Fallacy
   (d) Availability Heuristic

(a) 49. The value function exhibits all of the following features except

   (a) it is symmetrical
   (b) it does not have absolute value functions
   (c) it is asymmetrical
   (d) its slope decreases as it approaches its endpoints

(c) 50. Assume that a person wishes to purchase a car. Because he can only afford to spend $9000.00 on the car, he eliminates any car costing more. Next, he looks at how many doors the car has. Preferring a new two-door car he eliminates all four-door cars and used cars. Which of the following does the scenario describe?

   (a) additive strategy
   (b) lexicographic strategy
   (c) elimination-by aspects strategy
   (d) compatibility principle

(d) 51. One tries to discover a hypothesis consistent with a body of data according to

    (a) deductive reasoning
    (b) conductive reasoning
    (c) the verification strategy
    (d) none of the above

(a) 52. According to cognitive psychologists, a concept represents

    (a) the set of attributes shared by members of a class
    (b) a category of identifying aspects of a set of objects
    (c) a set of attributes unique to a member of a class
    (d) a category of conjunctive features

(c) 53. The statement "Learners generate hypotheses to express the relation between stimuli and labels and then test their hypothesis against the data" is an instance of the following type of reasoning

    (a) conjunctive
    (b) generative
    (c) inductive
    (d) deductive

(b) 54. According to researchers concerned with knowledge representation, a prototype represents

    (a) a unique member of a category
    (b) the typical features of the members of a category
    (c) the member of a category that is most readily recognized
    (d) the member of a category that occurs most frequently

(d) 55. How people categorize objects depends on their age. Adults

    (a) group objects by physical similarity rather than in functional terms
    (b) group objects in functional terms
    (c) try not to group objects because there tend to be significant exceptions
    (d) base feature inference on category membership rather than on physical similarity

(b) 56. Levine's blank trial procedure reveals that

    (a) subjects usually formulate one hypothesis at a time and shift it when a new attribute is given.
    (b) subjects usually maintain several hypotheses at a time and tend to shift hypotheses when one is disconfirmed.
    (c) subjects have trouble shifting to or creating new hypotheses
    (d) subjects have great difficulty in solving a problem if their hypothesis is disconfirmed

(d) 57. The essence of formal logic practiced by logicians and mathematicians is formed by

   (a) meta-cognitive reasoning
   (b) elaborative reasoning
   (c) inductive reasoning
   (d) none of the above

(d) 58. The statement "The probability of 2 events occurring cannot exceed the probability of one of those events" describes the

   (a) if-then law
   (b) basic rule of probability
   (c) conduction rule
   (d) conjunction rule

(c) 59. We generally believe that airplane crashes occur more frequently than they really do because much publicity is given to them. This is known as the

   (a) salience heuristic
   (b) base-rate heuristic
   (c) availability heuristic
   (d) common heuristic

CHAPTER 15

(c) 1. Memory traces can easily be changed by information learned after an event, even though we are not necessarily aware of the subsequent information. This is known as

   (a) the good subject effect
   (b) eyewitness failure
   (c) the suggestibility effect
   (d) the encoding event

(b) 2. In an example of source confusion, an eyewitness is likely to

   (a) believe a policeman over a stranger
   (b) remember everyone at a crime, not just perpetrators
   (c) believe in their own suggestibility
   (d) use memory enhancement

(a) 3. Leading questions should not be allowed in courtrooms, because the resulting answer may be erroneous. Information supplied after an event observed by a witness can cause changes in testimony, because

   (a) subjects are easily influenced by additional information
   (b) subjects believe what lawyers tell them
   (c) stress prevents encoding

(d) subjects aren't warned about suggestibility

(d) 4. Rehabilitation techniques have been used by neuropsychologists with a variety of patients. They have found treatments that work in training amnesic patients, prospective memory loss and in attentional deficits. One theme that occurs in cognitive rehabilitation is:

    (a) Retraining must take place soon after injury
    (b) Damage to only one hemisphere produces little impairment
    (c) Cognitive skills are generalizable to several domains
    (d) Performance tends to be domain specific

(c) 5. Cognitive rehabilitation seeks to use intact cognitive abilities to modulate impaired functions. To be successful the training should be

    (a) done while the patient is in the hospital
    (b) considered only in conjunction with medication
    (c) long lasting and ecologically valid
    (d) designed for classroom usage

(b) 6. Cognitive engineering would play a factor in

    (a) designing computer simulations of brain patterns
    (b) design the demands of a job to match human performance patterns
    (c) building models of animal migration paths
    (d) coordinating the right and left hemispheres

(b) 7. Applied cognitive psychologists have developed the concurrent task paradigm to assess an operator's performance in two tasks executed simultaneously. Which of the following is not true for the concurrent task technique

    (a) it reflects the limitations of working memory
    (b) it is typically used to track performance in actual work settings
    (c) it provides an opportunity to record the trade-off between two tasks
    (d) performance data from this task are typically recorded in POC curves

(c) 8. The POC curve expresses

    (a) signal detection performance as a function of false alarms.
    (b) speed and accuracy of a response.
    (c) performance in two tasks executed both individually and concurrently.
    (d) performance in two concurrent tasks.

(d) 9. Human performance researchers have introduced the "oddball task" in order to

    (a) assess the response speed and accuracy of pilots in simulated cockpits.
    (b) measure operator performance in two target tracking tasks executed individually and jointly.
    (c) record ERP patterns to an oddball stimulus presented according to a random schedule.

(d) record changes in ERP patterns resulting from an intermittent secondary signal presented as the person engages in a primary task.

(d) 10. The inventor of the typewriter arranged the keys in order

    (a) to minimize the finger distance between the typing of the most frequent letters in English print.
    (b) to speed the total typing time for standard samples of English text.
    (c) to facilitate learning of the keyboard.
    (d) to satisfy mechanical constraints.

(a) 11. Researchers have studied users' performance with different word processing editors. They found that

    (a) interference between different editing systems is negligible.
    (b) there is considerable interference between different editing systems.
    (c) there is positive transfer between different editing systems.
    (d) there is negative transfer between different editing systems.

(c) 12. Klahr and Carver (1988) investigated the effect of learning the LOGO language on skill in other problem solving domains and found that children

    (a) had acquired a specific LOGO skill that did not transfer to non-programming tasks.
    (b) had learned a programming skill that was transferable to programming other languages, but did not transfer to non-programming tasks.
    (c) had learned a general debugging skill that they could transfer to other tasks.
    (d) had acquired a debugging skill that helped them in learning the computer language Pascal.

(b) 13. The term "phonemic awareness" refers to the knowledge that

    (a) specific phonemes correspond to the letters of a language.
    (b) words consist of sounds.
    (c) utterances consist of separate words.
    (d) beginning readers acquire as a result of the phonics method.

(c) 14. Phonemic awareness

    (a) is usually acquired before a child enters kindergarten.
    (b) is important in storing word meanings.
    (c) develops as the child becomes a reader.
    (d) is a pre-requisite to reading instruction.

(c) 15. Another term for encoding is

    (a) retrieval
    (b) storage
    (c) decoding

(d) none of the above

(b) 16. The fact that children recognize words without explicit reading instruction supports

(a) phonemic awareness
(b) the Whole Word method
(c) automaticity of encoding
(d) none of the above

(a) 17. Select the reading method that emphasizes the alphabetic principle on which printed English is based

(a) phonics
(b) word integration
(c) comprehensive reading
(d) b and c

(b) 18. The goal of teaching problem solving skills is to

(a) categorize efficiently
(b) achieve the level of autonomous processing
(c) memorize more information
(d) a and c

(b) 19. A configuration of knowledge about an object, event or procedure is best described as

(a) description
(b) schema
(c) category
(d) a and b

(d) 20. Bahrick (1984) studied the retention of Spanish in subjects who had graduated college fifty years ago. He found that _____ was the most influential on retention.

(a) length of time without practice
(b) IQ scores
(c) amount of practice
(d) original training

(a) 21. Shepherd evaluated the Frame System in several experiments on face recognition. He found that

(a) for non-distinctive faces there was a decrease in recognition accuracy with increasing position
(b) after each trial recognition became more accurate
(c) recognition accuracy increased with a larger number of pictures
(d) recognition accuracy decreased with a larger number of pictures

(c) 22. Eyewitness testimonies are often inaccurate as a result of every reason except

   (a) witnesses are often stressed
   (b) witnesses are fearful of weapons
   (c) witnesses often do not encode the information into long term memory
   (d) witnesses are asked leading questions

(c) 23. Warrington and her colleagues tested 600 patients with brain lesions in their right and left hemispheres. They found that lesions in the right hemisphere are associated with

   (a) lower verbal scores
   (b) lower spatial scores
   (c) lower performance scores
   (d) none of the above

(b) 24. Posner and his colleagues tested subjects on the spatial cuing task. The results indicated that

   (a) the target was detected faster in invalid trials
   (b) the target was detected faster in valid trials
   (c) there was no difference between valid and invalid trials
   (d) the target was recognized faster for invalid trials for patients who had experienced a trauma to the parietal lobe

(c) 25. Human factors psychology is also known as

   (a) cognitive science
   (b) applied cognitive psychology
   (c) cognitive engineering
   (d) industrial psychology

(b) 26. Examinations on Performance Operating Characteristics curves indicate that when two tasks are executed jointly,

   (a) performance on one task diminishes
   (b) performance on both tasks diminishes
   (c) performance on both tasks remains the same as if they had been executed one at a time
   (d) one cannot perform either task

(a) 27. Eye fixation patterns are an example of

   (a) a behavioral measure
   (b) a physiological measure
   (c) a secondary task
   (d) extended practice with dual-task execution

(a) 28. The oddball stimulus paradigm is an example of

    (a) a behavioral measure
    (b) an ERP measure
    (c) a Performance Operating Characteristic
    (d) the phonics method

(d) 29. Which of the following invented the QWERTY keyboard?

    (a) Dvorak
    (b) Remington
    (c) Norman and Fisher
    (d) McGurrin

(b) 30. In research on word processors, experimenters found that the best device(s) used to position a cursor in a word processor environment was/were

    (a) the arrow pointing keys on a keyboard
    (b) the mouse
    (c) the joystick
    (d) specific keys on the keyboard

(c) 31. The first major level computer language written was

    (a) Binary
    (b) Logo
    (c) Fortran
    (d) Basic

(c) 32. Klahr and Carver (1988) experimented with children and their use of the programming language Logo. Based on their research, they concluded that

    (a) children were able to learn to program in computer languages
    (b) children enjoyed finding bugs in programs
    (c) children learned debugging Logo and applied it to other problem-solving contexts
    (d) children could figure out how to debug a program after having learned the general rules of Logo.

(d) 33. Phonemic awareness is

    (a) the ability to hear a sound from far away
    (b) the knowledge that syllables are made up of letters
    (c) the knowledge that sentences are made up of words
    (d) the knowledge that words are made up of sounds

(a) 34. In learning to read, a child comes to an implicit understanding of certain abstract concepts about language. Which of the following is not one of these concepts?

    (a) syllables consist of letters
    (b) utterances consist of separate words
    (c) there is a correspondence between letters and sounds
    (d) words consist of sounds

(c) 35. After many debates on the optimal method of reading instruction, researchers have come to the conclusion that

    (a) the whole-word method and the phonics are equally effective
    (b) the whole-word method has an advantage over the phonics method
    (c) the phonics method has an advantage over the whole-word method
    (d) neither method is satisfactory

(b) 36. Which of the following is not a stage in the acquisition of procedural knowledge?

    (a) the cognitive stage
    (b) the structural stage
    (c) the autonomous stage
    (d) the associative stage

(a) 37. Schemas are mental representations that

    (a) contain procedural knowledge
    (b) produce Performance Operating Characteristics
    (c) facilitate reading instruction
    (d) are essential for face recognition

(c) 38. Bahrick and Hall (1991) conducted research on math performance over a lifetime. They examined math proficiency as a function of all the following predictor variables, except

    (a) rehearsal activity
    (b) gender
    (c) the time it took to finish the test
    (d) the time that had elapsed since the subject's last math course

(b) 39. Bahrick (1984) also conducted research on the retention of Spanish learned in high school. Their results indicated that the retention interval affected retention the most. The next important factor was the following.

    (a) the time elapsed since the subject's last Spanish course
    (b) the amount of original training the subject had in Spanish
    (c) the amount of rehearsal the subject had when studying Spanish
    (d) the amount of time the subject had spent rehearsing Spanish since her last Spanish course

(d) 40. Bahrick chose the following term to label the bedrock of knowledge stored in memory over the years

   (a) long term memory
   (b) declarative knowledge
   (c) fundamental knowledge
   (d) permastore

(b) 41. Research by Geiselmann and his colleagues on eyewitness testimony suggests that recall was the best in this order:

   (a) hypnosis, the cognitive interview, the standard interview
   (b) the cognitive interview, hypnosis, the standard interview
   (c) the cognitive interview, the standard interview, hypnosis
   (d) the standard interview, hypnosis, the cognitive interview

(c) 42. Difficulty in naming a familiar object can result from a lesion in all of these, except

   (a) Wernicke's area
   (b) the angular gyrus
   (c) the medulla
   (d) Broca's area

(a) 43. Lesions in the following region are associated with lower verbal scores on verbal performance tests

   (a) the left hemisphere
   (b) the right hemisphere
   (c) the cerebellum
   (d) none of the above

(d) 44. Schacter and his colleagues suggested that rehabilitation from amnesia was more likely to be effective if

   (a) the job is broken down into small steps
   (b) each subtask is taught explicitly
   (c) the laboratory task simulates the work task closely
   (d) all of the above

(b) 45. In his study of eye fixations of airplane pilots, Fitts discovered that the mean eye fixation times on gauges in the cockpit was 600 milliseconds. According to Chapter 5, this is about

   (a) twice as fast as in reading
   (b) twice as long as in reading
   (c) twice as fast as in driving
   (d) twice as long as in driving

(a) 46. Which of the following is a typical job of cognitive engineers?

    (a) to improve the design of software so as to make it easier to use
    (b) to study brain patters of pilots
    (c) to devise new advertising techniques
    (d) to study the effects of cigarette smoking on ERP patterns

(d) 47. Which of the following invented a keyboard with only ten keys so as to eliminate the time interval of moving fingers between keys?

    (a) Norman and Fisher
    (b) Remington
    (c) McGurrin
    (d) Conrad and Longman

(d) 48. In America, light switches are turned upward to turn the light on, and downward to turn the light off. In England, the opposite practice exists. According to Chapter 15, this example represents a case of

    (a) practice
    (b) permastore
    (c) interference
    (d) compatability

(b) 49. According to Mayer, which of the following aspects of a computer language is the most difficult to acquire?

    (a) the vocabulary
    (b) conceptual knowledge
    (c) the format
    (d) the addition command

(a) 50. Klahr and Carver (1988) taught children the Logo programming language as a part of an experiment on transfer. They conducted their study to evaluate Seymour Papert's hypothesis that

    (a) there is a transfer of training between computer languages and other skills
    (b) children learn computer languages faster than do adults
    (c) children readily acquire debugging skills
    (d) conceptual knowledge of computer languages is more difficult to acquire than vocabulary

(b) 51. Landauer criticized cognitive psychology because it cannot be used widely in the workplace. He considered cognitive engineering as a discipline still in its infancy. Which of the following criticisms does Landauer not make about cognitive psychology?

    (a) cognitive psychologists study variables that illuminate abstract principles rather than concrete applications of their experiments
    (b) cognitive psychologists should concentrate more on learning computer languages than on studying abstract processes
    (c) designers do not understand what cognitive psychologists have been investigating
    (d) cognitive principles do not affect machine design

(b) 52. In problem-solving tasks, schema training is important and useful because it

    (a) helps to monitor one's own progress toward the solution
    (b) facilitates appropriate problem representation
    (c) involves examples of phonic instruction
    (d) treats faces as jigsaw puzzles

(c) 53. Which of the following is not mentioned in Chapter 15 as a retrieval mnemonic?

    (a) the encoding specificity principle
    (b) report of the witnessed events in a variety of orders
    (c) a line-up presentation
    (d) recall of the series of events from different perspectives

(c) 54. Bahrick and Hall (1987) experimented on retention of 50 English-Spanish word pairs. Subjects were placed into one of three training groups, an immediate, a one-day, and a thirty-day training group. Their findings suggest that

    (a) the immediate group exhibited the best recall level 8 years later
    (b) the one-day group exhibited the best recall level 8 years later
    (c) the thirty-day group exhibited the best recall level 8 years later
    (d) there was no difference between groups